W9-BZC-700

Canyon Solitude

A Woman's Solo River Journey
Through Grand Canyon

Patricia C. McCairen

Adventura
BOOKS
A SERIES FROM SEAL PRESS

Copyright © 1998 by Patricia C. McCairen

Canyon Solitude is an Adventura Book published by Seal Press. All rights reserved. No part of this book may be reproduced in any form, except for the quotation of brief passages in reviews, without prior written permission from Seal Press. Seal Press, 3131 Western Avenue, Suite 410, Seattle, Washington, 98121. sealprss@scn.org.

Cover design and interior Grand Canyon map by Clare Conrad
Cover photograph by Larry Ulrich/Tony Stone Images
Text design and composition by Laura Gronewold

Library of Congress Cataloging-in-Publication Data
McCairen, Patricia, 1940-
Canyon solitude : a woman's solo river journey through Grand Canyon / Patricia C. McCairen.
1. Rafting–Colorado River (Colo.-Mexico) 2. McCairen, Patricia, 1940- –Journeys–Colorado River (Colo.-Mexico)
3. McCairen, Patricia, 1940- –Journeys–Arizona–Grand Canyon.
4. Colorado River (Colo.-Mexico)–Description and travel. I. Title.
GV776.C63M33 1998 917.91'320453–dc21 98-11518
ISBN 1-58005-007-7

Printed in the United States of America
First printing, April 1998
10 9 8 7 6 5 4 3 2 1

Grateful acknowledgment is made for the use of the following previously published material: Dell Books for lines from *Illusions: The Adventures of A Reluctant Messiah*, copyright © 1977 by Richard Bach. Little, Brown and Company for lines from *Deep Water Passage: A Spiritual Journey at Midlife*, copyright © 1995 by Ann Linnea. *Outside* magazine for lines from "In the Canyon" by Edward Abbey, copyright © 1980 by Mariah Publications Corporation. Excerpt from *Women Who Run With the Wolves* by Clarissa Pinkola Estés, Ph.D., copyright © 1992, 1995 (p. 91). All rights reserved. Reprinted by kind permission of the author, Dr. Estés, and Ballantine Books, a division of Random House. Random House/Pantheon Books for lines from *Tracks: A Woman's Solo Trek Across 1,700 Miles of Australian Outback,* copyright © 1995 by Robyn Davidson. St. Martin's Press for lines from *The Wind in the Willows*, copyright © 1995 by Kenneth Grahame. Lines from *Another Wilderness: Notes from the New Outdoorswoman,* edited by Susan Fox Rogers (Seal Press) copyright © 1994, 1997 by Susan Fox Rogers. Lines from *Solo: On Her Own Adventure,* edited by Susan Fox Rogers (Seal Press) copyright © 1996 by Susan Fox Rogers.

Distributed to the trade by Publishers Group West
In Canada: Publishers Group West Canada, Toronto
In the U.K. and Europe: Airlift Book Company, Middlesex
In Australia: Banyan Tree Book Distributors, Kent Town

To Marian, who understood

Acknowledgments

Thank you to Faith Conlon, whose belief in my work made it a reality, and to Diane Sepanski, who meticulously corrected my grammatical mistakes. Thank you especially to Jennie Goode, whose patience, encouragement and editorial insight helped improve the quality of this book. And finally, thanks to all the people who turned down this Grand Canyon trip, thus giving me the opportunity to experience the canyon on my own and absorb all the lessons I needed to learn.

Contents

GRAND CANYON

COLORADO RIVER

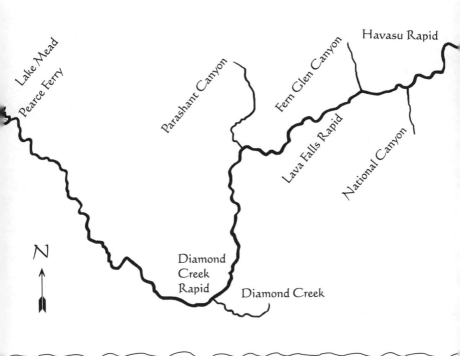

Lake Mead

Pearce Ferry

Parashant Canyon

Fern Glen Canyon

Havasu Rapid

Lava Falls Rapid

National Canyon

N

Diamond
Creek
Rapid

Diamond Creek

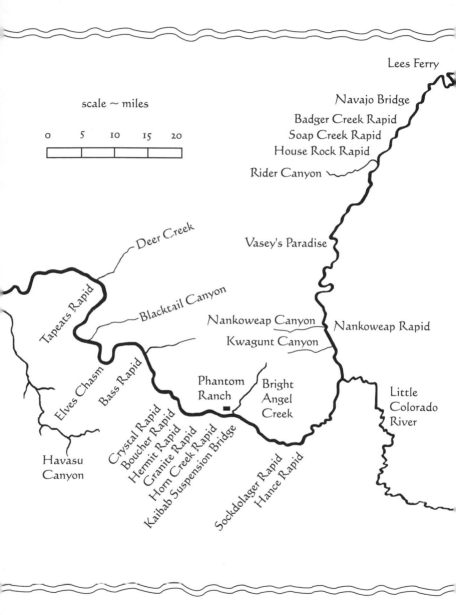

scale ~ miles

0   5   10   15   20

Lees Ferry

Navajo Bridge

Badger Creek Rapid

Soap Creek Rapid

House Rock Rapid

Rider Canyon

Vasey's Paradise

Deer Creek

Tapeats Rapid

Blacktail Canyon

Nankoweap Canyon

Nankoweap Rapid

Kwagunt Canyon

Elves Chasm

Bass Rapid

Phantom Ranch

Bright Angel Creek

Little Colorado River

Crystal Rapid

Boucher Rapid

Hermit Rapid

Granite Rapid

Horn Creek Rapid

Kaibab Suspension Bridge

Havasu Canyon

Sockdolager Rapid

Hance Rapid

Canyon Solitude

1

On the Edge

Security is mostly a superstition. It does not exist in nature, nor do the children of men as a whole experience it. Avoiding danger is no safer in the long run than outright exposure. Life is either a daring adventure or nothing.

— *Helen Keller*

I scramble upward, moving around tufts of bear grass, yucca and prickly pear cacti that cling to the steep talus slope. I stop, listen to the melodic notes of a canyon wren's song, then look up and spot a rock affording an inviting handhold a foot above my head. As I do whenever I'm about to grab on to something beyond my line of vision, I wonder if a rattlesnake lies curled on top of the rock. Would the surprise attack, the pain of the poison-filled fangs, cause me to lose my balance and plunge down the hill to the pile of rocks

3

below? I shake the vision from my mind's eye and grasp the rock, test its reliability and flinch when it pulls free and hurtles by, inches from my face.

When I started out from the river corridor to explore this side canyon an hour ago, I ignored my customary fear of climbing by focusing on thoughts of bighorn sheep making the same ascent, making it often enough that they are probably responsible for the trail being in such an impossible place. I only wanted to hike, not climb, to quench my curiosity about a previously unexplored tributary of the Colorado River. With another two moves I stand perched on a small mound a hundred feet—or so it seems to me at this moment—above the floor of the canyon. I turn my head slowly and look behind me, down the trail I have just ascended. It falls away at a dizzying pitch. I return my gaze straight ahead. The trail that I have followed with childlike faith continues on the other side of a crevasse. All I have to do is take one giant step from my slim purchase to a narrow, slanting shelf covered with small stones.

I inhale deeply, filling my lungs with desert air. A cool breeze wafts up the canyon, reminding me that the day is getting ready to snuggle under the cover of night. Darkness will settle in this canyon before it reaches the river. I curse my heedless scramble up a slope to nowhere, I wish for wings, I long for the comfort of the flat, sandy beach back at the river. If I were skilled at this sort of thing, or fearless, or had more presence of mind, I wouldn't be stuck on a ledge at the bottom of Grand Canyon paralyzed by fear. The same fear that has kept me stuck in life so many times before, afraid to move forward, to take a step that would free me from the ordinary, the mundane, the insufferable. A crippling fear that deadens my potential and limits my relationship with the world. It's so easy to cling to the familiar, even when it's deplorable.

My legs begin to quake like aspen in a breeze. The more prolonged my inertia, the more impossible the step appears. I'll die. That's it. I don't have a chance. The fall will fling me off the cliff face onto razor-sharp rocks below. With the specter of my body being torn apart, a shrill squeak escapes my throat, followed by another, and still another.

I know I can do it. I've taken more difficult steps in life, chosen pathways that required more of me than this single step. Like deciding to raft the Colorado alone.

I remain frozen, hating the canyon's inhospitality, its

exacting lessons that ultimately teach me more about myself than the natural world it contains. On impulse I leap forward, plant one foot firmly on the ledge and will it to hold against gravity, to hold in spite of the loose pebbles sprinkled over the surface. Another step follows quickly, and another. Barely daring to breathe, I inch forward until I'm on flat, solid rock slabs twenty feet wide. Tears flood my eyes and for a moment I cry, each sob releasing the terror I had known only a moment before. A few minutes later, I wipe my eyes and start back down the side canyon via an easier route, back to the beach on the Colorado River where my raft is secured. The canyon has spared me once again.

2

Initiation

There are some moments in life that are like pivots around which your existence turns—small intuitive flashes, when you know you have done something correct for a change, when you think you are on the right track.

— *Robyn Davidson*, Tracks: A Woman's Solo Trek Across 1,700 Miles of Australian Outback

The drive across the high desert of northern Arizona between Flagstaff and Lees Ferry, the put-in for Grand Canyon river trips, is 137 miles. It can take as little as two and a half hours or as much as four, depending upon driving style and condition of the vehicle.

It's late afternoon when we leave Flagstaff. Later than I want. I need to be at Lees Ferry now, not four hours from now. Dee, my companion, doesn't care. He's just along for the ride, so the anxiety is all mine. I press the accelerator of my heavily laden truck to the floor. It coughs in protest as we near the crest of the 7,282-foot pass that puts Flagstaff behind us. The dry October air, scented with pine, slaps my cheek through the open truck window and braces me with its cool, crisp freshness. Stately ponderosa form a dense barrier between the highway and the San Francisco Peaks, like sentries guarding the rooftop of Arizona. High above the forest, a red-tailed hawk sails on the thermals that come off the peaks, moving only the tips of her wings to remain aloft. Not a movement is wasted, not a feather is out of harmony, as she glides on unseen tracks of invisible motion.

As Highway 89 begins its descent, my truck picks up speed, leaving the ponderosa behind on the slopes of the mountains. Piñon and juniper replace the tall pines for a while, until the lack of water causes them to give way to the empty land and endless space that dominate the Colorado Plateau. By the time we cross the Little Colorado River, we've dropped three thousand feet in elevation.

This is Navajoland, parched with thirst and nearly barren of trees, people and animals. Occasionally a sign announces the existence of a town, which usually consists of nothing more than a gas station and a general store selling Navajo rugs, jewelry and a few sundry odds and ends. Now and then a hogan off in the distance, roadside stands, a skinny horse, dot the landscape. It is a land that holds nothing and everything: a stark terrain replete with subtle beauty that evokes spiritual consciousness.

From inside the truck, the turning of the wheels is like minutes ticking away on a clock, each revolution propelling me closer to the onset of my journey. I grip the steering wheel tightly in an attempt to quiet the nagging voice that questions the wisdom of setting out to raft the Colorado River alone—an impetuous decision, born of loss and despair, one that on serious reflection would probably be abandoned as easily as a winter coat on the first day of spring. River running is a group endeavor: In the past sixty years only a handful of people have traversed the fluvial pathway of Grand Canyon alone. Of that handful, only one was a woman—and she took her trips in the early fifties, when the river was warmer than it is today.

I'm not out to set records, I tell myself, though I admit I'm intrigued by the possibility of being the first woman to solo the canyon without portaging any of the rapids. But all that is secondary. The need to resolve the unresolvable questions of my life is what drives me into this vast canyon. And into my soul.

I glance at my companion. His long legs, bent at right angles, attest to the lack of room in the cab of my pickup. A beard, not fully grown in, covers his lower face, and a visor shades his eyes. Brown hair streaked with sun-bleached blond and traces of white falls haphazardly over the visor's strap and covers his ears. Dee is a river guide on the Colorado, one of the many who combine the romanticism of an Old West cowboy with the sensitivity of a New Age mountain man. Instead of bucking broncs he wrestles bucking rafts. After my departure, he'll drive my truck back to Flagstaff where he lives, then meet me at Pearce Ferry, 280 miles and twenty-five days downriver.

Three hours into the drive the road twists and turns, still dropping in elevation. On the far side of a barely discernible fissure, the vermillion cliffs blaze a fiery red in the late afternoon sun. Sand hills rise on either side of the highway. I push gently on the brake pedal, slowing to the twenty-five miles per hour posted on a warning sign. Two more signs declare in informative and demanding tones: YOU ARE LEAVING NAVAJOLAND and NO STOPPING ON

PAVEMENT. I slow to a crawl.

Dee asks, "What color is the river?"

Before I can reply, I drive onto the edge of a narrow suspension bridge. Four hundred fifty feet beneath the curved steel structure, the Colorado River flows peacefully through the chasm it carved.

Dee leans out the truck window and peers over the railing. I repeat his question back to him, "What color is the river?"

"Not enough light down there to tell," he replies, then adds, "but I think it's green. At this time of year you could have clear water all the way."

The Colorado River is released from the bottom of Glen Canyon Dam, fifteen miles upriver from Lees Ferry, making the water an unnatural, though beautiful, dark green. Only when it rains and side creeks flood, carrying in red, silty mud, does the river return to its natural *colorado*.

After crossing the bridge we turn right onto another narrow, winding road. A sliver of moon follows in the sun's path. Five miles later I slow and come to a stop. Moving placidly past the Lees Ferry launch ramp, the Colorado shimmers in the final rays of sunset as it appears from around a bend out

of the last of Glen Canyon's sandstone walls. On the opposite shore the bank, hidden by a thick growth of tamarisk
trees, fronts low sandy hills behind. Downstream, Kaibab
Limestone ascends out of the left bank like a grand staircase,
while on the right, beige sand hills flow in waves up to the
vermillion cliffs.

The scent of the river, full-bodied like a good wine, mixes
with the sweetness of the tamarisk trees and greets me as I
step from my truck. I walk to the edge of the river and crouch,
dipping my fingers into the forty-five-degree water. I shudder, then shake off the drops of water, sprinkling myself with
memories.

I was born on the Colorado River at the bottom of Grand
Canyon, thirty-five years after my initial birth in New
York City.

The conception took place on the South Rim in front of
the El Tovar Hotel with my first sight of that ragged, rough-
edged cutout. Nothing in this world could have prepared
me for the immensity, the changing colors, the contours of
rock upon rock that lay sprawled out in front of me. It had

to be an illusion. I leaned over the edge of a stone wall, erected to protect fools from sailing into the abyss, to take a closer look. A slight breeze played with the ends of my hair. Far below, a zigzag line revealed the course of the Bright Angel Trail. When the trail straightened out, it entered a haven of cottonwood trees at Indian Gardens before vanishing into the Tapeats Sandstone on its way to the river. Minuscule hikers and a mule train inched through red dust. Above a butte, its pinnacle a thousand feet below me, a raven, wings spread wide, rested on a current of air, as comfortable in her domain as I was awed by it. I followed her flight with my heart and eyes, soaring over hard rock and prickly brush to immortality.

When evening's light cast long shadows, I wandered along the South Rim trying to understand what I was seeing and to comprehend the changes that were beginning to explode inside me.

The intensity of my feelings threw me off balance. I had chosen a canyon trip on the recommendation of someone I barely knew. While suffering from dysentery in Nepal the previous autumn, I declared to an American companion that I would take my next vacation in the United States, where I wouldn't get sick. She suggested a river trip through Grand Canyon. She said it was fun; I took her word for it. My boating experience was limited to trips up the Hudson River or a ride on the Circle Line around Manhattan. I had never slept under the stars and did not comprehend the meaning of whitewater. None of my friends were interested in joining me, and so as I often did, I went alone. Knowing nothing more than what I had gleaned from the vague descriptions in the company's brochure, I decided on a partial trip—I didn't want to spend all my vacation time on something I might not enjoy.

The following morning I woke as the sky danced through its roll call of orange, pink and yellow. I stumbled across uneven ground in the dark and cold until I found a small group of people huddled together.

"Is this the meeting place for the river trip?" I asked.

"I'm not sure," a man answered. "The brochure said to meet at the head of the Bright Angel Trail, but there's not enough light to see where the trail begins."

I joined them, hoping I had found the right group, and that someone would come along soon and give us directions.

She arrived with a coffee pot, orange juice, granola bars and sweet rolls. "Hi, everyone, I'm Sue."

"Give me a minute and I'll read off your names," our hostess said. She was far too cheerful for either the hour or the temperature. "Meanwhile have some breakfast. This coffee will take away the chill and wake you with a jolt."

"I know it's hard to believe," Sue began after she had identified us, "but it's going to get very hot very quickly, so we should be getting on the trail right away." She packed the remainder of the breakfast in the back of a beat-up truck, hefted a large, square, black rubber bag onto her back and set off. She was out of sight before the rest of us had put on our packs.

The first half-dozen switchbacks proved the warning signs at the top of the trail were right. This was no Sunday stroll through Central Park. The five flights of stairs to my East Side apartment hadn't prepared me for the narrow, steep, dusty trail. My pack weighed me down, the straps rubbed my shoulders and dug into my waist. My thighs and knees begged for relief, and rivulets of sweat trickled between my breasts and soaked the back of my shirt.

If I was fascinated by the canyon from the rim, I was

totally overwhelmed the farther I descended. From the top it was a beautiful panorama, but within, the towering, multi-colored walls embraced me in a fundamental reality. My hand grazed over the texture of the Coconino Sandstone; my back rested against the polished faded rose of the Redwall Lime-stone; my face burned from the heat waves radiating off the keen-edged ebony of the Vishnu Schist. The solidness of it all steadied my footsteps, cleared my mind, calmed my apprehension.

Sue went from the front of the group to the rear, looking after each member and urging the slowpokes to move faster. She carried her bag easily, as if it weighed nothing, though I suspect it was heavier than mine and certainly a lot more cumbersome.

"What's in the bag?" I asked.

"Tonight's dinner—twenty-five steaks and ten boxes of fresh strawberries," Sue answered, before making her way to the front of the group.

She nearly ran down the trail; only duty to us held her back. "My boyfriend Dave is leading this trip," she said. "We haven't seen each other in a week. It's the longest we've been apart since we met last fall."

I smiled. Only love could drive someone to hike seven miles down a rugged trail with a bagful of steaks and strawberries.

At the bottom of the trail, the river was waiting.

I removed my pack and felt myself rise off the ground. With effort, I focused on a smooth rock beside the river and walked toward it. I lounged on it as if it were as soft as an armchair. After a few minutes I removed my boots and slowly submerged my feet. The cold was shocking, then relieving. Drops of water flew around me as one of the other hikers filled her hat and poured icy water over herself. She gasped with pain and pleasure.

We sat by the river, the passage of time marked by the buzz of flies, the song of the canyon wren and the cramping of tired muscles.

Then, silently, four large oar-powered silver pontoon rigs, looking like Viking ships to my impressionable mind, slid toward the waiting group. When they touched shore they came alive with people—jumping off, tying up, throwing black rubber bags on the sand. Two bearded men dressed in shorts and dilapidated tennis shoes set up a table in the shade of a cliff that sent heat waves into the 110-degree air. Layers

of ham, turkey and pastrami, cheddar and jack cheese, tomatoes, onions, lettuce and sprouts, loaves of whole-wheat bread,
mayonaise, Dijon mustard and salsa, along with cookies, apples
and oranges, quickly appeared on the table.

"Luuunnnch!"

The sound ricocheted off the walls and wrapped itself
around the group, drawing us to the table.

Peter, the smaller of the two lunchmen, attempted to regain order. "Take it easy now. Let these folks covered with trail
dust go first. Otherwise they might run over the rest of you."

Some people stepped back and I found myself at the side
of the table packing everything I could between two slices
of bread. I sat on a rock in the shade and devoured it.

Across the stretch of sand, standing on top of a flat boulder, Sue gazed into the eyes of a tall, muscular riverman with
a thatch of light brown hair falling over his forehead. They
stood motionless, eyes locked. After a very long kiss they
parted and Sue went up the trail carrying the same black
bag. I wondered what she had in it this time.

Dave approached the group and spoke in a soft, patient
voice that flowed over us with the consistency of velvet sliding over a manicured hand. "We try not to let it happen, but

people do get hurt on these trips." His brows dipped and he stroked his beardless chin. "We've never actually lost anyone that I can think of. If you fall into the river, relax and keep your mouth shut. You'll get tossed around a bit, but your life vest will bring you to the surface. Don't get between the raft and a rock, or under the raft either. And don't panic. We'll pick you up as quickly as possible. It's probably more dangerous on shore than it is in the boat, or in the river. When you're off the boat, keep an eye out for rattlesnakes and scorpions. We're uninvited guests in their home, and they get a bit cranky if you step on them or put them on with your clothes. Shake everything out before you put it on, and look under trees and overhanging rocks before you get out of the sun, because they're trying to do the same thing."

Dave glanced behind him at the waiting boats. "It's time to go now. Tighten up your vests and get aboard. We'll fill you in on things as we go along."

I selected the last space on a boat with five elderly passengers and a Tom Cruise look-alike at the oars. First names were flung out, and in a parental way everyone advised me to hang onto a rope running down the center of the raft. I preferred to stand up and look around to see where we were going, but I complied. Minutes later we dove into the trough of a wave. Before the raft rose again, everything in it was covered with water. *Wet!* I did not expect to be so wet! The raft dipped and rose, dipped and rose. Something within me snapped. With each motion I screamed—not a cry of fear or pain but of utter joy, released enthusiastically, naturally. I was vulnerable and open and totally happy. I was a child again, uninhibited, wild and free, riding a roller coaster with the excitement and anticipation of hanging on the brink before plunging down the near-vertical slope. As the water calmed I leaped up, threw back my head and shouted at the top of my lungs: *"This is fantastic!"*

We camped on a fine sand beach that night, spreading out and relaxing in as many ways as there were people: Gail wrote in her diary, John recorded the river's voice, Phil went off to meditate, Peter played his flute, Ingrid sketched. I lolled on the beach, wiggling my hips and shoulders until the sand and I were a perfect match, while I observed the subtleties of light on my Mother River, my Father Canyon.

When the kitchen crew called dinner, we filled ourselves with the special-delivery steaks, corn on the cob, potato salad and fresh strawberries sitting on Dutch oven biscuits, smothered in whipped cream.

Eight days flew by—eight days with twenty-odd strangers, riding rafts through enormous rapids, sleeping under stars, hiking up side canyons, swimming in pools. We laughed and sang and teased each other and played like children, though some were over sixty-five and others barely twenty-one. On the eighth night, after all the rapids were behind us, we tied the rafts together and floated on a silvery slip of river beneath a moon and stars that bathed us in enchantment.

A plane ride later I was back in New York, back at my customer promotion job with Air France, eager to tell everyone stories of my Grand Canyon trip. My friends and colleagues looked at me in wonder, perplexed by my reaction to a week's vacation. I tried to explain and came up short. Descriptions of the canyon, the rapids, the waterfalls and the people elicited a lukewarm response.

I began to think they must be right. It was just another trip, not even particularly exotic. I had already traveled to more than twenty countries on four continents and could obtain a free ticket to any corner of the globe whenever I wished. Each year I spent a weekend in London, longer weekends in other European cities. This had been my first domestic vacation in years. I had good friends, a rent-controlled apartment in New York City and a stable job that gave me access to the world. On weekends I biked around Central Park or joined a Sunday volleyball game. During the week I often grabbed an inexpensive meal and twofer tickets to a Broadway play. I had already been with Air France for nearly seven years. This was the time to think of stability, working toward a higher position, a good income and retirement, not to daydream about a river trip.

The weeks passed. I expected the memory of the trip to fade, my life to return to normal. But the wildness and freedom I had touched upon so briefly continued to haunt me. Something deeper had happened, something I didn't understand. A stranger had emerged in the canyon, and she fought to remain present. I tried to stuff her back wherever she had come from but she wouldn't have it. Babe had been born on the river and she demanded attention, she insisted on recognition. Each night she took me back to the towering cliffs and icy green river. Babe didn't want to be a sexy girl with bleached blond hair, makeup and short skirts to show off legs that turned men's heads. She didn't want to smile all the time, whether she was happy or not, and never speak about feelings, especially negative ones. She didn't care about being acceptable to others or pleasing men at her own expense. She threw fits at living in a box. She terrified and beguiled me at the same time. Babe had a vitality I hadn't known I possessed, and she was disrupting my well-ordered life. Like a newborn screaming in her crib, she demanded nourishment and attention.

Then one day, for no particular reason, a remark by Peter, the philosophical head cook on the trip, popped into my head: "Most people are too afraid to give up their security to do what they really want." It was all my new self needed. She grasped that simple, straightforward observation and ran with it. Ran from the high-rise in Manhattan to the rivers of the West and a tipi on Colorado's high plateau.

3

Going Solo

Among shadows, things appear larger than they really are.
— *Sherry Simpson, "Where Bears Walk" in*
Another Wilderness: Notes from the
New Outdoorswoman

Dee and I survey Lees Ferry. No one else—not a ranger,
other boating parties or fishermen—occupies the
pebble-strewn shore that leads into the Colorado River.

In midsummer Lees Ferry is a hubbub of activity. Boatmen and women, dressed in colorful shorts, T-shirts and swim-
suits, rig a variety of boats, tie on gear and shout friendly
greetings to other guides. By evening things have usually
quieted down, as small groups of people eat a cold dinner or
drive up the road to Marble Canyon Lodge for a hot meal.

Shortly before noon the following day, buses pull up and disgorge people into the blazing sun. They eagerly approach their waiting launch, firing questions at their guide with the velocity of a machine gun. By early afternoon all the trips have left—just in time to make room for the following day's group.

In the quiet dusk, Dee and I work slowly, enjoying the solitude of a familiar place. I inflate my boat while Dee continues to unload my truck, spreading the equipment out along the ramp. Darkness encompasses us completely after the raft is inflated. I place a plywood board on the floor of the raft, cover it partially with a red checkered tablecloth and set a candle to one side. Sitting on opposite sides of our makeshift table we spread out a modest picnic supper.

A slight breeze causes the candle to flicker and we both move to protect the flame from going out. The moon sets and millions of stars send pinpoints of light out of the black sky. The horizon is a jagged silhouette; the river speaks with a soft murmur as it laps gently against the shore. Dee tells stories about growing up in the desert.

Then he shoots a question out of the blue: "Patch, how'd you get the Park Service to let you do a solo trip?"

⌒⌒⌒

The National Park Service requires a permit to run the Colorado River through Grand Canyon—the most sought-after permit in the river world. As a result, thousands of people compete for a spot on the river, and the Park Service has tried numerous ways to make the system fair. Shortly before my solo trip, they instituted a waiting list by holding a lottery and assigning people a number. Luck was with me—I was near the top of the list and had to wait only a year for my permit. Less fortunate boaters had to wait up to ten years for their permits. The waiting list is still in effect, but in the mid-nineties the Park Service imposed a yearly twenty-five-dollar fee to remain on the list in an effort to purge the list of frivolous overloading. While it's difficult to obtain a permit to run the Grand, it's even more challenging to put a trip together.

A year before my scheduled trip date, I asked friends to join me. Most felt it was too far in advance to make a commitment. I waited and asked again, and asked others when those first ones declined to go.

I hung on tenaciously, and as the put-in date drew closer,

I spent much of my time on the phone contacting everyone I knew who I suspected might enjoy a canyon trip. Answers varied but the result was the same:

"I'm sorry but I have to finish this house I'm building before winter sets in."

"I'd love to go but I can't take four weeks off from work."

"I've done too many Grand trips this year." (Is this possible?)

"I don't have the money."

Genuine excuses that discouraged and depressed me. Fifteen days before departure I waited to hear from one remaining person. If he declined, the trip would have to be canceled. That afternoon I received his postcard: *Definitely cannot go on your trip. Family business.*

I sat at my desk holding the card, tears streaming down my face, and stared at a poster of boats floating on still water in Grand Canyon. Like Alice stepping through the looking glass, I transported myself inside the photo. The recollected scent of water and tamarisk trees, of sun-drenched rocks and sand, engulfed me. For a brief moment, I was at the bottom of Grand Canyon, until I realized I had lost my chance, perhaps my last chance, to be there—unless I did the trip alone.

I doodled on a blank piece of paper. Words, sketches, scribblings flowed down my arm and onto the paper. *A solo trip would be exciting . . . definitely a challenge . . . too preposterous to even consider . . . a ridiculous dream . . . the Park Service would never let me do it.* I flipped the paper into the waste basket.

I swiveled my chair around and opened a carton filled with files. Finding the one I wanted, I extracted a set of papers: *National Park Service Noncommercial River Trip Regulations.* I scanned it and stopped. A sentence jumped out at me: "Single boat and solo trips must be approved by the Canyon District Ranger."

I looked at it in disbelief—except I already knew it was there. Months before, when I first glanced through the regulations, that sentence stood out. The Park Service had never included it before.

I decided to call. It wasn't really a decision at all. It was a whim. I dialed casually, removing myself from the question at hand. I was simply curious. There must be a mistake.

The phone rang two or three times. A woman's voice answered: "Grand Canyon National Park."

"May I speak to the District Park Ranger, please?"

"May I ask who is calling?"

Of course you can't! I gave her my name.

"Just a moment." The line was quiet. Then, a muffled greeting.

"Is this the District Park Ranger?"

"Yes, this is Larry Van Slyke," a soft male voice said.

"I have a private permit for an October 19 trip. I haven't been able to get anyone else to go, and I was wondering what you would think about me doing a solo trip?"

"Alone?"

"Yes." My voice was barely audible.

The line was quiet. I couldn't even hear him breathe.

Then, without any noticeable change in his voice, he said, "Why don't you tell me about your experience."

With a burst of courage I went over my years of professional guiding. I told him about the six Grand trips I had already done and the dangers I saw in doing the river alone. My voice was steady, though I was talking a little too fast to sound truly confident. I finished by telling him I was fully aware of the risks involved and felt I could handle them. It was a lie. I hadn't even thought about them before that moment.

Larry chatted with me, asking a few questions. His manner

was light and easy. He could have been asking about a recent movie I'd seen. I knew the questions were important, but I couldn't remember my response the moment after I'd answered. Another part of me had taken over and was reacting to this man in a sensible, appropriate manner.

He stopped. The tone of his voice changed slightly. "You seem to know what you're getting into, and I think people should have that option."

I pressed the phone to my ear, stunned by his words. He was allowing me to carry out this crazy scheme of mine. He should have said no. He was supposed to protect me from myself.

"I'm not entirely positive I'll do it. A solo trip only occurred to me today. Before I really weigh the consequences, I wanted to be sure you would approve."

"When do you think you'll know?" He seemed a little anxious over my hesitation.

I thought quickly. It was Tuesday. Put-in was exactly two weeks away. "By the end of the week," I answered with more confidence than I felt.

"Please call me one way or the other. I'll need to notify people that there will be a solo trip down there."

"Okay. I'll call Friday at the same time."

Agony! The agony of trying to decide something that could affect the rest of my life. The difficulty of looking into the future, weighing unknown consequences against unknown odds. Fifty times a day I swung from one side to the other. At breakfast, lunch and dinner. During a phone conversation, I was suddenly mired in the throes of deciding my fate. Whatever I was doing slowed to a snail's pace. I couldn't shut my mind off. My stomach churned and formed an ever tighter knot as I progressed further into a world of imagined catastrophes.

Visions of disaster haunted me, shocking me during the day, waking me during the night. Rapids grew to monstrous proportions, waves towered over me and foaming fingers of white reached out and tossed my boat around like a matchstick. Swept along by the river, I was out of control, drifting farther and farther from my boat until finally I abandoned all hope of reaching it. Stranded on shore, I huddled against the inhospitable walls, chilled to the bone and on the edge of exhaustion. I was dying in the depths of Grand Canyon.

I walked to the store. In the middle of a step the sidewalk changed to sand, the buildings to canyon walls. It was night. A huge drop of water pelted me, then another and another. Flashes of lightning pierced the darkness. In the distance, a deep-throated growl swelled with each passing second. I listened, puzzled by the sound. Then, a moment later, a moment too late, huge boulders pounded down on me; red liquid mud engulfed me, sweeping me along in its relentless path.

I lay in bed and stared into the dark. Suddenly I felt a movement. I turned my head and looked into the malevolent eyes of a rattlesnake. Her tongue flickered, testing the air. A faint rattling, only slightly louder than the pounding of my heart, paralyzed me with fear. The snake struck. Her fangs plunged into my neck.

When I shook off the images, I questioned my sanity, my ability, my ego. What qualified me to consider rafting the Colorado River alone? Was I really as capable as I wanted to believe? If everyone thought I was crazy, would that dissuade me? How much of my ego was tied up in doing this trip? Was even part of my decision based on wanting the approval of others? After my visualizations, the questions I couldn't answer and the doubts, I decided not to go. It was too great a risk. I could lose my life.

My heart sank. I wanted to do the trip desperately. But alone?

I turned back to the fears, dissecting them one at a time, looking at them thoroughly like a medical student studying a cadaver. When I looked at each fear rationally, it was not the demon I originally made it out to be. Rafting the canyon alone was possible, perhaps even reasonable. In seven years of running rivers all over the West, I had seen only one or two rattlesnakes, and never near my bed. The same applied to scorpions. I had seen two flash floods, both from a safe distance. And I had flipped my raft once, mostly because I was inexperienced and had my boat loaded improperly. When analyzed logically, there seemed nothing to fear. With my emotions rising to a high, I decided to do the trip.

But, what if . . . ? My high slipped away. One by one the fears took over. I grabbed hold, catching my departing rationality by the tail, and went over all the arguments once again. I went through this process over and over—during every waking hour and in my sleep. I began each day thinking about nothing else.

Friday morning brought nothing new. There was no

sudden revelation, no burst of courage. It was simply that the despair of staying proved greater than the fear of going.

I dialed the Park Service.

"Hello, Larry, this is Patch. I've decided to do the trip—alone."

He answered in a steady, unemotional voice, "Okay, I'll notify the ranger at Lees Ferry that one person will be showing up."

I hung up. *No!* I reached for the phone. All I had to do was explain that I was suffering from lunacy and wouldn't go after all. My hand rested on the receiver, trembling slightly. Then I pulled it away and stood up. I had a lot to do.

Clear, clean action took over, carrying me along with its momentum. One step followed another, logically, progressively. I made lists of things to do and things to buy, crossed them out, made new lists and began the slow process of organizing logistics. Priorities changed. Amounts of food, briquettes, garbage bags and toilet paper attained significance. For the moment, it no longer mattered if I was crazy or sane, normal or weird. I planned and shopped and packed. Boxes, bags, lines, frames, decks, packaged food, tarps, tent and a variety of other paraphernalia filled the backyard.

The bustle of activity kept me from thinking, and if the reality of what I was doing slipped into my consciousness, I quickly pushed it aside. I was determined, but I had to hang on to that determination with a tight grasp or I might succumb to the frightened little girl who still lived within me and filled me with doubt. Even Babe had difficulty maintaining a calm, confident manner.

I wasn't sure I wanted to go alone, but I had no intention of allowing just anyone to join me. Too many inharmonious trips in the past had taught me to be particular when choosing river companions. I also had no intention of dealing with anyone who might pose a logical objection. No doubt everyone I knew would think me insane. A barrage of good reasons for not taking my trip might be more than I could withstand. There might even be a certain amount of relief if I allowed friends to stop me. I could be released from the awful burden of responsibility I had placed on myself. It would be *their* fault I didn't go. Their choice, not mine. I had only given in.

I avoided everyone.

Then, one evening while I was preparing dinner, my housemate Marian and her friend Thad passed through the kitchen on their way out. I took exaggerated interest in stir-ring my soup. They stopped.

"Hi, Patch. Making dinner, huh?" Thad asked.

"Yes." I stirred faster.

"Soup, huh?"

"Yeah."

"Looks good."

"Easy."

"Easy is right." He shifted from one foot to the other and smiled. "How're you doing?"

"Good." I glanced away from the soup wondering what might come next. I turned off the burner.

Then, with only a trace of curiosity in his voice, Thad asked, "You have a Grand trip soon, don't you?"

I flushed. "Yes." I avoided meeting his eyes, hoping to discourage further questions.

He did not take the hint. He lingered. His interest had been piqued. He was a boatman with a love for the canyon, hoping to work there the following season. "When is your put-in?"

"October 19." I could've left it there. Suddenly I had an uncontrollable urge to talk about the trip. "I'll leave here the fourteenth and do my last-minute shopping in Flagstaff. Then I'll go up to the ferry the day before." I waited expectantly for the next question.

"How many people are going?"

"One." It slipped out casually.

A heavy silence settled over the room. The refrigerator hummed as if it too were nervously awaiting a dreaded reaction. I glanced at them. Marian's mouth dropped, her eyes opened wide with shock. Thad's face was as vacant as a ballpark in winter.

They were the first to know. In the few remaining days before I left, other friends asked the same questions, in the same order. Men were intrigued, women scared. Men expressed envy and a desire to do a solo trip themselves. Women expressed fear, advising me to latch on to another trip. Inadvertently, I had aroused the respect and admiration of men. I wanted it from women. I wanted their support, a sisterhood that encouraged us to break away from dependence. I didn't get it.

On the eve of my departure I sat at my desk, writing a note to Marian. Random images raced through my mind. A lingering thought of death. Did I have an *Appointment in*

Samarra? If I don't make it . . . Yes, that was a possibility, not just some random phrase written for its shock value. *If I don't make it . . .* do this and that and something else. It was a reality. Death could call on me. It may be more dangerous crossing a city street than spending twenty-five days alone in Grand Canyon, but the perspective was different. It was the aloneness of it. Facing whatever there was to face alone.

The first gray light of dawn moves into my sleeping bag. A restless wind accompanies it, urging me to rise. Looking straight up I come face to face with Orion, his sword drawn. To the east a faint glow tints the sky behind the last of Glen Canyon's walls.

Rising up on one elbow, I look at Dee. Only the top of his head is visible. I lie back, snuggling into the cocoonlike warmth of my sleeping bag. I close my eyes and try to relax. I open them again. I'm anxious to begin doing something, anything, to keep from lying in my bag and thinking about all that needs to be done. Restlessly, I turn over and come face to face with a deflated tube.

"Oh, no!" I bolt upright, carrying my sleeping bag with

me. "I have to repair my boat before I even begin my trip."

I look over at Dee, hoping my commotion has not disturbed him. Two green eyes blink back at me. I smile at them. They respond by closing. I dress and head toward the bathrooms at the top of the parking area.

When I return, Dee is up.

"My raft has a leak," I say. "I'll have to patch it immediately."

He yawns and walks to the soft tube. Putting his thumb over the valve, he twists the stem until it closes properly. "Good morning," he says with a smile.

"Good morning to you too." I look at him sheepishly but he takes no notice.

"There's a million things to be done," I say. "I should get started right away."

He nods and sets out a cold breakfast.

Dee relaxes against the tube of the raft. The sun climbs over the canyon wall and smiles down on us. With its arrival I shift into high gear. I leave Dee and go from one thing to the next, accomplishing nothing. The day is slipping away and I'll never complete everything that needs to be done before departure.

In an easy manner, Dee suggests we move the raft closer to the water and tie on the frames. His composure provides a steadying influence. My jitters abate a little.

My raft, an Avon Professional, is my prized possession. She's my link with the wilderness, with wild and tame rivers, with peaceful days and beautiful memories. She handles easily, holding steady through waves that tower above us, pivoting cleanly around rocks. She has carried me down a variety of rivers and brought delight to "first-timers." This fifteen-foot-long, seven-foot-two-wide craft is the Rolls Royce of boats. Her gray nylon hypalon fabric resists wear, though a couple of patches on her underside confirm the fact that she's not invulnerable to sharp rocks or jagged tree branches. A few weeks ago, in a fit of sentimentality, I painted a rising sun on the bow along with her name, *Sunshine Lady*.

Dee and I place two frames made of contoured metal tubing inside the raft and tie them securely with tubular webbing, popularly known as hoopie, to D-rings on the side of the boat. The frames provide a rowing seat from which I can control the raft, along with deck space on which to put the mountain of gear I'm taking with me.

Turning away from *Sunshine Lady*, we nearly collide with

two men prowling through my gear like inquisitive cats. Baseball caps shade creased faces that appear to be pushing sixty, and potbellies stretch out the fabric of their plaid shirts. They hold fishing rods, a tackle box and a six-pack of Coors beer.

I look at them suspiciously.

"Hi, how are you today?" Dee asks.

"Okay," the larger of the two men answers with a slight drawl. "You goin' down the river?" His deeply lined face is serious but friendly. He looks at Dee, awaiting a reply.

"She's going." Dee motions toward me with a hint of a smile on his face.

"Well, aren't you goin' too?" The lines deepen, the voice grows indignant.

"No, she's going alone," confirms Dee.

"Alone! You're goin' to let her go alone!?"

"Yes," Dee answers, smiling at me.

"Humph!" The second man joins in, looking directly at Dee. "What kind of man are you, letting your woman do whatever she wants? You're supposed to take care of her."

The first man shakes his head and comments more to himself than to us, "What is this world coming to?" Then for the first time he acknowledges my presence. "You take care of yourself, young lady."

"I will." I camouflage my own indignation with a smile.

The two men walk away and Ranger Jon arrives, looking official with clipboard and pen in hand. He checks out the raft, first aid and repair kits and everything else the Park Service requires for a trip through Grand Canyon. When Jon signs the permit approving my departure, I leave him and Dee and begin tying my equipment in place. I work alone until nothing is left on shore and nothing remains untied. Hours have passed. The pit of my stomach is hollow. I go over to Dee and sit next to him on the ground.

"That's it, I'm ready," I lie. My seat feels rooted to the earth. A chill raises goose flesh along my arms. Long, wispy cirrus clouds hide the sun, allowing only faint rays to shine through, too weak to provide warmth.

"Before you take off, will you let me try your boat out?" Dee asks.

"I expected as much." I'm happy for the delay.

With some effort we push the boat into the river. Dee climbs aboard and rows away from shore. He turns the raft around in both directions, then rows back to me.

"It handles beautifully," he proclaims. "It's so nice and light."

If I didn't feel so anxious, I'd sling a smart remark back at him. The best I can do is cast a skeptical eye over his six-foot-two frame.

I shift nervously from one foot to the other. I've come this far and have lost all sense of control.

As if reading my thoughts, Dee says, "You can still turn back."

I study my feet and shake my head. It's not possible to look him in the eye.

Dee and I hug. His bigness feels warm and secure. Without emotion, I turn and climb aboard my raft. Taking up the oars I quickly pull away from shore until the current grabs my boat. The river is wide and green and deep, stretching out endlessly in front of me. A tight knot of fear clutches my stomach.

I look around. Dee walks over to the fishermen who have their lines in the water. I wave. Three arms rise and wave back.

"I'm really doing it," I say softly to myself, afraid someone might hear. "Yes, I'm really doing it."

My raft moves quickly away from Lees Ferry. I wave again at the three men, who have become specks in the distance, and take some comfort in the limited contact. Then, turning, I look ahead toward the first riffle, feeling very small and insignificant.

4

Mother River

"So—this—is—a—River."
"The River," corrected the Rat.
"And you really live by the river? What a jolly life!"
"By it and with it and on it and in it," said the Rat. "It's brother and sister to me, and aunts, and company, and food and drink, and (naturally) washing. It's my world, and I don't want any other. What it hasn't got is not worth having, and what it doesn't know is not worth knowing. Lord! the times we've had together . . ."

— *Kenneth Grahame,* The Wind in the Willows

Solitude has a sound all its own, a feeling, a special vision. With each stroke on the oars, I draw myself deeper into its realm. This solitude differs distinctly from the times I've spent alone in my home or walking through the woods by myself. Hesitantly, I sample it. Otherworldly, risky, fascinating. Intimidating, serene, vulnerable. Yes, I'm terribly small and vulnerable, minuscule compared to this deep, green river and the walls growing up around me.

The canyon is familiar, yet strange, like an old friend under new circumstances. An imperceptible inner excitement pulsates through my veins, compelling me to absorb every impression I feel, hear, see. My senses sharpen, taking me beyond myself, beyond my fears, into another world. Within two miles of Lees Ferry, the well-known walls have risen quickly on either side of a river that has wedged itself between solid rock. The vermillion cliffs are gone, hidden behind Kaibab Limestone that sits on top of the Toroweap Formation. The rest of the world has disappeared. It is just the canyon, the river and me. To be here, that is all there is. Nothing more is necessary. Nothing more exists.

Complex designs created by the walls cracking and breaking under great pressure form filigree patterns; a cactus growing out of a crevice in bare rock illustrates survival under sparse conditions; a rock balanced on the edge of a precipice waits for the right moment to fall. Not if, but when. Sometime in the next million years, or a moment after I pass.

I hold still and listen. The river gurgles as it plays around a rock; a birdsong penetrates the silence with sharp, sweet notes, then stops. Silence upon silence.

Abruptly, the quiet is terminated by a sudden movement. Startled, I look around and see a pair of ducks take off, squandering energy in their haste to flee. Then, with a quack that undoubtedly says, "Wait for me," a third duck follows. They land within sight downstream, and as I approach, take off again in the same formation: first the couple, then the lone duck. This is repeated three or four times, until I begin to hope they'll accompany me on my voyage. But the next time I draw near, they circle overhead and fly back upstream.

I sweep my oars through the water, pushing on one while pulling on the other—a Double-Oar Pivot, in rafter's language. The stern, or rear of the raft, now faces downstream, and I look upstream. I glance over my shoulder, line up the boat in the direction I want to go and pull evenly on both oars.

Rowing is a clean action, unadulterated in its purpose or movement. In flowing, flat water with no upstream wind, the relaxing, repetitive rhythm has a meditative quality to it. Lean forward, dip blades in water, lean back, pull; lean forward, dip blades in water, lean back, pull. Over and over and over.

I glance over my shoulder again. Navajo Bridge is in sight. The "what color is the river" bridge. The only motorized crossing of Grand Canyon. It looks farther away from down below than the river looked from above. I pivot the raft and face downstream toward the bridge. The rhythm of my rowing takes on a new character. My body remains fairly still while my arms move forward at opposite ends from one another in a circular motion, so that one blade enters the water as the other enters the air. Portegee: a useful stroke, though not as powerful as pulling.

I study the bridge carefully. Have our times coincided? My heart leaps and I smile. A small yellow truck creeps slowly across the steel structure. Midway, Dee leans out the window, arm raised high, waving back and forth. I return the wave, eagerly trying to close the gap between us. In a minute he is gone. A few minutes later the bridge is behind me, and solitude closes in once again.

Now I am truly alone. It is the aloneness of the wilderness, starkly real and present—I can no longer even look forward to a glimpse of my friend. The next place I can expect to see anyone is Phantom Ranch, eighty-three miles and seven days downriver.

"This is it," I say out loud. "Another Grand trip, another few weeks between the walls." Elation takes shape deep inside me and rises like a bubble seeking the surface of the river, bursting forth in laughter that evolves to love as I stare at the river. *The* river. A green, brown, chocolate, red, clear, silty, raging, tranquil ribbon of energy. The river is everything: nothing more, nothing less. A power that courses through the artery of the canyon, transforming, converting, quietly and slowly, steadily and persistently. Powerful even in tranquility. Powerful even when tamed by humans. A power that is there by its very existence. Not a greedy, controlling power, but one to be respected, a power of an entity so complete, so self-contained, it has no need of another.

She is a power that teaches those who open themselves to her. Her lessons may be subtle, or frightening. She cares not if we learn: It is up to us to seek her out. I have chosen to join her here in her home. The pupil coming to the mentor, the lover to the beloved, the searching soul to the guru. The child returning home to her mother.

Changing, changing, constantly changing, she casts a rhythmic, sensuous spell. A sleek, beautiful goddess, alluringly seductive, forgiving to those who love her, dispassionately indifferent to those who do not. Lovingly she folds herself around a rock, teasingly she laps at the shore, stroking and caressing it, forming and molding it to her desires. Playfully she gurgles, laughing and talking to whoever will listen. As late afternoon arrives, her surface sparkles. Bedecked in a million diamonds, she dances a sunlit dream lost in ecstasy. In the flash of an instant she is capable of creating a bubbling, intoxicating happiness or a frustrating helplessness, the highest exhilaration or the deepest, darkest fear.

She vacillates in these first few miles. Slowly she swirls around, swinging one way, then another, crossing from shore to shore, ambling upstream, then down, losing the thread of her current so that I must dig deep with my oars to keep from aimlessly strolling with her. In this languid state she entices the uninitiated into a false sense of confidence, beguiling them with the belief that they are more powerful than she and nothing she does will affect them. I know better, for I have seen her in her fury, or just simply playing in her own mysterious way. Without a moment's notice her mood changes, and suddenly she leaps high into the air, crashing over and around boulders, flinging herself on them with wild abandon and an ebullience that can be unsettling. She dances with excitement, enjoying her display of potency, enticing me to join in her play. Then just as abruptly, she settles down, heaving and churning as if breathing deeply after her great exertion. Once again she flows with a gentle nonchalance, encouraging me to forget the display she put on only moments before.

I surrender myself to her and, in so doing, gain strength. Now, drifting alone in my little boat, I pray to her and the canyon gods to be kind and allow me to pass unharmed.

I grab the oars and pull in earnest. I need to make miles and chase away the October chill that steals energy from my bones. Even without a watch, I know it's late afternoon, and the place I want to camp is still four miles away.

Dark green water slips under my boat. Soon I hear the rumbling of Badger Rapid. As the noise grows louder, my skin tingles in familiar anticipation. I look over my shoulder. The river disappears over the rapid's steep drop, leaving me viewing a straight, horizontal line. Occasionally a spray of white jumps high above the line, inviting me to play.

In the 277-mile length of Grand Canyon there are approximately seventy-five named rapids, plus numerous riffles. Sometime in the past, someone rated the rapids on a scale of one to ten, ten being the most difficult. An accomplished boatman I know claims that a rapid is nothing more than water running downhill over rocks. Zen or denial? I'm not sure. I do know that too much fear or not enough can create confusion, so that anything can happen and often does.

I glance quickly at the guidebook lying on top of the load. At this water level Badger is rated a six. I tuck everything away and, to gain height, stand up on the boxes tied directly in front of my seat. Meticulously, I study the rapid, gauging the nuances of the current. I float closer, still standing, until I'm near the brink. A touch of adrenaline adds a keen edge to my senses. Then in one motion I hit the seat, grab my oars and align *Sunshine Lady* between two breaking waves. Four- and five-foot standing waves follow. She rises just enough to keep from taking on water, feeling solid and steady with the weight of the load in the bow. In less than a minute I am at the bottom of the rapid. I pull over to a white sand beach.

A sandbar estate waits to be settled. It's large enough for a party of twenty-five or thirty, so I have ample space to furnish it as I wish. I decide upon a place for the kitchen and bedroom, change my mind and decide upon another. The novelty of being in my first camp alone adds an element of excitement to an otherwise mundane chore. I find a level place and set up my tent. When it is erect, I unpack my Therm-A-Rest mattress, releasing the valve so it will inflate itself. Next I unroll my sleeping bag and arrange the cotton sheet liner inside it. With everything ready for the night, I open a waterproof bag and pull out dry clothes. Cotton and wool hug my chilled skin.

I walk back to *Sunshine Lady*. It's time to set up the kitchen. I grab a plywood board that serves as a rear deck and screw four two-foot lengths of pipe into the deck's flanges. A moment later I have a table. I then place two twenty-millimeter ammo boxes next to the table. The heavier one contains my entire kitchen commissary—pots, pans and utensils—while the lighter box holds staple items—flour, honey, tea, oil, powdered milk, matches, and so on. I rout around a box or two still tied on the raft and take out a quick and easy meal.

With dinner started, I level out a place in the sand upwind of the table for a firepan and go in search of fuel. The beach is strewn with driftwood, and within half an hour I have more than enough wood for the night and following morning. I start a fire and sit next to it while I fill the empty cavern in my midsection. The late afternoon sun burns the canyon walls crimson.

A fire, hot food, a cozy tent and a warm bed—this is my home for the night. River runners, backpackers, adventurers of all types know how to create an instant home, as snug and restful as any permanent structure. All true wanderers can quickly set up lodging that reflects both their personality and their familiarity with a wilderness setting. Though we may have a dwelling elsewhere to contain our everyday life, this is the home of our soul.

The moment I leave the arms of Morpheus my apprehension rises. Still in my sleeping bag, I scoot across the floor of the tent to the door. The zipper releases easily and I look out on a clear blue sky. A cool autumn breeze grazes my face. Down the beach a line stretches taut between a log and my partially beached raft. The feeling of dread evaporates.

I reach behind me, pull clothes out of a stuff sack pillow and dress quickly in long underwear, turtleneck, wool sweater, pants and down vest. The canyon is colder than I expected. Certainly colder than I like. Better get used to it, I warn myself, it's only going to get worse. I grab my camera and walk north to the upstream side of Jack Ass Creek and the talus slope beyond.

The morning light reveals a miscellany of human sign. Unpleasant ones. Blackened rocks encircle partially burned debris. Beer cans, pieces of aluminum foil, pop tops, toilet paper and cigarette butts lie under low shrubs and are partially hidden behind rocks. The litter is an eyesore and a shock, for most of the canyon is pristine, even with more than sixteen thousand people traveling through it each year. Jack Ass Canyon, however, is easily accessible from the outside world, and this camp is often used by people hiking down the side canyon.

A well-defined trail leads through rabbitbrush, hackberry, verbena, blackbrush, evening primrose, Mormon tea and cacti—low bushes that come no higher than my waist and provide protection from a harsh summer sun for lizards, mice, scorpions and snakes. When the trail turns east to go up Jack Ass Canyon and out to the Navajo Reservation, I head north and drop down into a large, dry wash covered with small, smooth stones. On the opposite side of the wash I begin climbing up the Hermit Formation, a steep slope of soft red shale covered with large rocks that have fallen from the formations above.

About one hundred feet up I turn and lean against a solid boulder the size of a small car. The inner world of the canyon stretches out in front of me. The river flows almost directly south. In the morning light it is a small dark ribbon threading its way between lighter colored walls, disappearing into rock in the distance, and decorated with the white bow of Badger Rapid directly below me. Sunlight touches the western rim of Kaibab, turning it a light beige, while the eastern rim throws a dark shadow on the lower formations. Directly across the river, Badger Canyon's wide mouth yawns, its throat choked with boulders. On this side of the river, my camp is reduced to a few bright blotches against the subtle colors of the canyon. My eyes wander over the scene as my mind travels back to other rivers.

With Babe barely a year old and my worldly possessions reduced to a few boxes of books, basic kitchen equipment, a stereo, a bicycle and a variety of clothing, I headed to Oregon and a twenty-seven-day whitewater school.

Within five minutes of meeting the twelve other students and five teachers, I knew I had joined a unique group of people. Ages ranged from eighteen to fifty; lifestyles included a hippie, a scientist, an artist, a few students, a couple of secretaries and a Wall Street attorney; conversations reflected diverse interests and brimmed with undaunted vitality. Clothing from Third World countries and bargains found at secondhand stores were the fashion. Hair was long on women and longer on men, most of whom had not encountered a razor in a very long time. But the most distinctive quality was that each person possessed his or her own version of Babe.

We set up camp at Alameda Bar on the Rogue River, as different as a place can get from Grand Canyon. While the canyon paints a giant tableau of beige, rust and pink cliffs, the Rogue covers a canvas with the forest primeval. Thousands of pine, fir and spruce trees, along with a variety of oaks, alders and willows, climb the steep slopes of the canyon, and the river flows clear and shallow, moving swiftly around and over boulders that dot the center of the stream.

Excitement prevailed as we inflated seven rafts and packed five days of food in watertight boxes. Our guides—Rick, Julie, Stich, Bob and Gab—instructed us with humor and patience. We fumbled with hoopie until the essential bowline and half-hitch knots were mastered, then placed the boxes and waterproof bags in the available space on the rafts and tied it all down. By the time we took off, morning had disappeared into noon.

I joined three other students in Stich's paddle boat, prepared to conquer the river in a matter of hours. With an audacious confidence that blinded me to any possible danger, I volunteered for the job of paddle captain soon after we were on the river. It took me just minutes to run the boat up on a rock.

A lunchtime later, we pulled in above Rainey Falls. Scouting the falls, the group babbled louder than the river, louder than the thunder of the ten-foot sheer drop that spilled over a natural dam. The navigable alternatives to the unrunnable falls—a chute where boats are dragged and shoved over smooth river rocks to a calm eddy below, and a fish ladder which requires maneuvering a raft through a strainer of rocks, then lining it up in the chute, shipping the oars, and holding on as the raft careens down to the eddy—were barely given a passing glance.

We neophytes stood by the side of the falls, awed by its power. The fact that running the falls was pushing the limits of safety only made it more enticing. We waited for the final word from our guides.

"Let's do it," Bob said. Three of us joined him in a scramble over wet rocks to claim an empty twelve-foot raft. We carried the raft to the top of the falls, our faces pink with exertion and excitement. We discussed the best approach and took our positions, each gripping a paddle.

We pushed off and Bob yelled, "Paddle forward."

In perfect unison, we stroked the water with our paddles and moved the raft toward a glassy hump at the brink of the falls.

"Stop!" Bob commanded, and we held our paddles out of the water. He stood up and peered ahead.

"Forward!" We paddled together.

"Stop!" He turned the bow of the boat slightly to the right.

"Forward!" he screamed. "Hard forward!"

Four paddles dug into the water like spades into the earth and pulled hard. The boat sprang toward the falls. I jammed my left foot between the tube and the floor of the raft and braced myself.

"Stop!" Bob yelled.

We held our paddles out of the water, ready for the next command.

"Oh shit! Hang on!"

The world went dark. A frothy turbulence tossed me around like a dog playing with a rag doll. Stabs of pain shot through my left knee. I surfaced, gulped in massive amounts of fresh air and looked for the others. Directly in front of me, Bob climbed into the raft. When I yelled, he reached out. I gripped his arm and he hauled me into the boat.

"That was nasty," Bob said.

"You ran that pretty far to the right." Stich stood on the rocks nearby.

"I'll say," Bob replied. "I got lost on top. But looks like we all made it okay."

"I don't know," I said. "My leg hurts like hell. I can't straighten it."

"Are you sure?" Bob asked. He and Stich huddled next to me.

The three of us examined it. My knee bent at a right angle and twisted slightly to the side. They touched it gently. Pain shot through it. "I can't straighten it," I said again.

The rest of the group crowded around.

"Are you sure?" Bob asked again.

I tried to move it but the pain stopped me. I shook my head and leaned back.

For a moment everyone was quiet. Then Rick, the lead instructor, bent down and said in his melodious southern accent, "We'll have to take you to the hospital."

"I'll have Stich run back and get the van and drive it to Graves Bar, but we'll have to rig up a stretcher and carry you there. Do you think you can handle that?"

"Yes." I sighed. "I'm sure it's fine. The doctor will just straighten it out and then I can join you all again."

"I hope so. It could be broken," Rick said.

"No. I don't think it's broken," I said. "I've broken this leg before and this doesn't seem as if it's broken."

The only way out of the Wild and Scenic Rogue River, other than by boat, is via a narrow hiking trail. A makeshift splint was tied around my leg, and I was placed on a stretcher fashioned out of a tarp and two oars. Rick took charge. An entourage of eight men stood ready for his command. "We'll take turns carrying her. As soon as you're tired, give your handle to someone else. We'll make the best time that way."

I lay on the stretcher and studied the patterns the leaves

and conifer branches made against the clear blue sky. The stretcher rose and a gentle rocking motion ensued as the guys carted me up the trail. I felt like Cleopatra, but I wasn't enjoying the experience. My leg throbbed.

"How're you doing?" someone asked after a while.

"Fine. You're doing a great job. Thanks so much."

"It's okay. But I sure didn't expect this to be part of whitewater school."

"Neither did I."

They marched along quietly, changing hands frequently. As the trail got rougher, they became more verbal.

"Damn, she's heavy."

"Here let me take it."

"Naw, I can go a little farther."

"God, she's heavy."

"I think you'd better relieve me, Dave."

"Got it."

"Can you go a little slower, guys. I can't see my feet."

"Okay. Okay."

"Easy now, the trail is pretty narrow here."

"Damn, she's heavy."

"Would you stop saying that!"

"I can't help it."

"How're you doing?"

I looked at the face asking the question. "Just fine, but I wish I could make myself lighter."

"Don't listen to them. You're just fine."

"We've got to get her across this rock slide. It's going to be tricky."

"Take it easy now."

"Don't tip it. We don't want her to fall out."

I peeked over the side of the stretcher. The trail dropped fifty feet in a jumble of rocks to the river. I held my breath.

"Damn, don't tip the stretcher."

"There, that's better."

"I'm not sure how much farther I can go."

A moment later I was transferred into a waiting van and whisked to the hospital.

"You've fractured your tibia and fibula and torn the ligaments in your knee," Dr. Renaud said. "I'm putting you in a full-length cast. I may have to operate. You'll have to stay here at least a couple of days."

"Shit!"

Outfitted in a plaster cast and crutches, I joined the group when they came off the Rogue River. Though I had missed the first few days of the trip, I was welcomed into the extended family that had already developed. As planned, I stayed in camp while the others learned how to read water, row and paddle boats. Sometimes Gab, the shuttle driver, and I would drive to an overlook where we could watch their progress, and at other times I stayed in camp while he ferried people and boats back and forth.

Our caravan hit the road in an old school bus that had been painted white and towed a six-foot enclosed trailer that carried most of our gear. The excess was stuffed in the back of the bus or tied on the roof. We drove to various rivers in southern Oregon and northern California. At night the musicians in the group played guitars, harmonicas and spoons while the rest of us sang or hummed along. We read chapters from *The Wind in the Willows* aloud around a campfire, then painted scenes from the book on our bus and trailer. At times I indulged in self-pity, but after one particularly bad day, I made peace with myself. My plaster cast may have kept me off the river, but I learned to plan meals for extended trips, cook over a fire and bake in a Dutch oven, tie down loads, and repair rafts. Despite my broken leg, it was an extraordinary experience.

The school came to an end with a farewell dinner, liberally infused with hugs and kisses and tears. Later that summer, when my leg was rid of the cast, I learned to row and paddle. (Years after my horrendous run of Rainey Falls I made a second attempt in *Sunshine Lady*—this time successfully.)

I was hooked and, like a hub around which the spokes and rim of a wheel turn, my life revolved around whitewater rivers. I lived by the motion of the earth. Sunrise. Sunset. For months at a time, my only roof was the stars and the waxing or waning moon. My bed was a small pad and sleeping bag. My immediate possessions were stuffed in two small waterproof bags and an ammo box. During the winter months, the only job I would consider taking was one that would release me for the summer so I could continue my pursuit of flowing water.

After spending the winter and following summer in Colorado I moved to the Sierra foothills in California to work on the Stanislaus River, a nine-mile stretch of whitewater through an enchanting limestone canyon. It was possible to do the run in one day, though most of the time we took two days.

We managed to slow time down to a near standstill, examining the world around us in a way most people had never experienced before.

When not on the river, the guides lived on ten acres of land that included a ramshackle house with a checkered history that embraced cowboys, whores and Chinese laborers. It doesn't rain in California during the summer and most everyone slept outside on the ground, but those guides who stayed most of the year had an interesting assortment of homes. My Lakota tipi was set up in a private spot toward the back of the property. Lisa lived in a house nestled in the branches of a tree that looked as if it came straight out of *The Hobbit*. Carol resided on a platform ten feet above the ground where she read and wrote and played her guitar when she wasn't on the river. Then there was David's yurt, Marty's rickety old school bus that wasn't about to go anywhere and Sparky's converted school bus that made a lot of houses look shabby.

It was my first experience with group living and I thrived on it. I had all the privacy I wanted in my tipi and all the companionship I needed with the other guides. We usually ate together in the main house and discussed trips, our plans for the winter and a range of topics that covered everything from politics to psychology. We took saunas together, learned to juggle and walk a tightrope and played a lot of music.

Though my lifestyle was free and unscheduled, I was not without goals and dreams. I enjoyed the challenge of rowing and paddling increasingly difficult rivers. I traveled to Oregon and Utah, running other rivers, seeking to improve my skill at the oars or guiding paddle boats. I studied the water, watched other people, picked up ideas. I took my time, rarely approaching something beyond my ability until I was ready. I wanted to be good for my own pleasure, my own sense of satisfaction. And also to fulfill my dream of rowing professionally on the Colorado River.

I began this quest by sending a letter and résumé of my river employment history to one of the twenty companies that held concessionaire permits with the Park Service to run the Colorado River through Grand Canyon. They seemed the one most likely to hire me since I had worked with their parent company in other states, I already knew some of their boatmen and they were the only company at the time who considered hiring women.

My résumé and letter were never acknowledged. Later that same year I followed up with another letter. No response.

The next year I stepped up my writing campaign. My persistence paid off. In early spring the owner of the company called me and offered me a date for an assistant boatman trip. I was ecstatic. The apprenticeship went well, and after speaking to the owner at the end of the trip, my hopes rose quickly. My dream had just moved within reach—or so I thought.

My hopes remained high and I continued to be persistent. I called and wrote letters but gradually I had to accept the fact that I wasn't making any progress. At five foot, five inches I was too small to row the Colorado, they said. I found out later that one of the women already working for the company was smaller than I. Though I looked and felt ten years younger, I suspected that at forty they thought I was too old, though men my age had no problem being hired.

I received two more guest trips on the Grand, but with my dream shattered I stopped rafting commercially. I had put too much emotional energy into obtaining a job on the Colorado and hadn't left room for other options.

I glance down at my camp next to Badger Rapid and wonder if it was the right decision. My life is floundering, my goals are muddled. If I can't have the Grand, what else is there?

~~~

I point my camera at various subjects, I daydream, I sing softly to myself, and otherwise wile away the early morning hours.

When I return to camp the river is rising.

There is something absurd about being on a river that rises and falls every day like the ocean's tides. But unlike the ocean, the Colorado's fluctuations are neither consistent nor predictable. They can amount to a few inches or a number of feet.

Water is most often let out of Glen Canyon Dam in the morning and cut back at night, but Saturday and Sunday water is usually lower than weekday water, and there are regular exceptions to the release schedule. As I move downstream away from the dam, the time of fluctuation varies. To keep track of the water I have to calculate the number of miles I am from the dam, divide that by the speed of the river and add the answer to 9:00 A.M. This gives me the approximate time the water will begin its rise for the day.

When the river drops, it can beach boats, dangle them by a bow or stern line off a cliff and transform rapids from an easy run to a strainer of rocks. If it goes up, it can sweep downstream gear that was carelessly left on the beach, cause boats to tear out of their moorings or batter rafts against rocks. Some rapids grow in size and power with rising water, and a favorite camp can be hidden and completely washed away under the rising tide. I check *Sunshine Lady* and growl at the men who mess with Mother Nature.

I eat breakfast, clean up the kitchen, take down my tent, pack my bags, load the boat and tie on gear. By the time I depart I've done two or three hours of work. Floating the river is the easy part.

The morning—it could be afternoon for all I know—slides by on a mostly quiet river. At the bottom of Soap Creek Rapid the red Supai Formation rises dramatically out of the river. Horizontal slabs, deep rust in color, form ledges along the water's edge, some large enough to shelter a sixteen-foot raft. In twelve miles the canyon has grown from a negligible child to a massive giant, heaving fortresses of stone that resemble medieval castles high above the river. The river, pinched to half its original width, swirls and churns. Beaches are scarce, and only a few are large enough for more than a quick rest stop for a small group of people.

Sometime in midafternoon I stop for lunch at a tiny beach. The sunshine and stillness of the air heat up the sand and me in turn. With joy I take off my clothes and bask in the sun like a lizard.

I listen to an audible silence. Nothing moves, other than the river, running quietly and deep. Rocks and sand and flora stand as silent sentinels over the river. Without movement or sound they pervade the atmosphere with a powerful aura. They speak of a timeless existence, exuding an energy and a spirtualness that transcend human comprehension. Certainly they are beyond mine.

I rise from the sand that hugs my behind and put cheese and pickle relish between two slices of bread. The canyon watches over my shoulder. Its presence is everywhere. A dynamic presence. It is this intangible essence that lures me back time after time. The river rushing over rocks or swirling slowly in a deep pool, the late afternoon sunlight glowing on the canyon walls, the smell of rain, the sound of wind stirring the tamarisks or the silence that grows enormous when everything is still.

On each trip the canyon and river bewitch me beyond reason with unspoken visions of happiness, power, love, fear, perhaps even immortality. They cause me to do things I ordinarily would not contemplate, to believe things I otherwise would not consider. Another window opens, shedding light on some aspect of myself, sometimes subtly, sometimes blatantly. The canyon strips away the superficialities of everyday life, reducing me to the fundamentals of survival. Alone in the wilderness, I am forced to come face to face with myself until the layers of doubt and insecurity fall away and I reach the core of my being. The canyon's existence is pure truth. Traveling within it requires the same honesty.

House Rock Rapid is a menacing, ominous collision of water against rock. I stand quietly on the left bank overlooking the rapid. A shaft of sunlight filters through Rider Canyon on the opposite shore, lighting up a small portion of green water like a spotlight on a stage. Tranquility and turmoil bound side by side. Subtle sounds are drowned out by the turbulence of the river. My heart rate quickens, my mouth grows cotton, my stomach forms a knot. A fleeting thought sweeps through my mind: *So this is what it means to be alone.*

A fan of rocks thrown out by Rider Canyon during

numerous flash floods compresses the river's width in half, forcing the river violently against the sheer wall of the left bank. At the bottom of the rapid a large boulder has fallen off the left wall, creating a turbulent hole as the water pours over it. The only safe run is on a small channel between the hole and rocky shoreline on the right, making House Rock a difficult rapid to run.

I take a few deep breaths and head back to my boat, which is pulling on its line as if impatient to be off. A vision of *Sunshine Lady* tearing loose and floating off by herself flashes through my mind and sends a shiver down my spine. I pull her toward me, tuck the line away and climb in. Cautiously, I row up the eddy next to the wall, then turn the boat's stern toward the right shore and pull evenly and steadily across the current toward the center of the river. At the edge of the whitewater, I look down at the waves and holes and rocks that lie in front of me, picking out a path that will take me away from the surge of water going into House Rock Hole. With an energy generated by fear, I pull hard on the oars as the raft slips steadily to the left. I am sure to lose the battle; the river will win as she always does. Then an unseen current bouncing off the left wall snatches *Sunshine Lady* and slides her past the hole with inches to spare.

It is late afternoon, time to find an overnight camp. I pass one small beach after another. Each has its own charm so that I am tempted to stop and make it my home, but for some perverse reason I pass by, looking after each longingly as it disappears from sight. A lowered sun and a wet ride through a small rapid soon encourage me to stop at the very next camp. With a nearly human contrariness, beaches are suddenly in short supply. I float another mile, studying the banks on both sides of the river before I spot a flat ledge of fine white sand. I pull into the eddy and climb up a steep bank to the camp. My footprints are the only ones to mar the sand.

5

Solitude

*Solitude offers the greatest opportunity for the fine tuning
of our souls.*

— *Ann Linnea*, Deep Water Passage:
A Spiritual Journey at Midlife

S ometime in the early morning hours I wake. No sudden sound, no snap of a twig or animal rummaging
around in the kitchen disturbs me. Just the knocking of a
thought on the door of my mind.

With no tent between me and the stars that form shimmering patterns in the inky sky, I stare up at Cygnus and
Cassiopeia. Off to the east Orion does battle with Taurus the
Bull while the Twins and Seven Sisters watch. As cool air
tingles my face, I snuggle into my bag and laugh. I am light

and giddy and, most of all, free.

What a privilege it is to have the time, equipment and ability to raft the Colorado River alone. I do what I want, when I want, how I want. I dawdle around camp in the morning and choose my own pace on the river during the day. I hike side canyons that entice me and pass up those that do not. I dress without regard to style or appearance and undress when and where I want. There is no one with whom to discuss the day's plans, no one to insist on doing something I don't want to do. There is no one else to see, no one to comment, no one to criticize my actions and idiosyncrasies. Every choice of every moment in every day is mine alone.

I revel in my canyon solitude until I realize the freedom I pursue with a passion is connected to loneliness, rather than to the ties of companionship. I squirm against the notion, then think about the different group trips I've done. A couple of them were excellent; the group flowed together with a rapport that magnified the wonder of the canyon. One or two were downright bad, and much of the time was spent debating what to do and how to do it. But underlying each one, good or bad, I felt awkward, never certain I was doing the right thing, never quite fitting in.

Even when I was praised I wondered if the person meant it, and when there was discord I might argue my side, but it left me unnerved. If I won the argument, I felt guilty and fretted about upsetting the others. I worried about what I had done wrong and what was wrong with me, and why I couldn't express what I wanted without displeasing everyone. A pang of fear would hit the pit of my stomach, and I'd slip off to be alone and nurse my wounds while everyone else presumably had a good time.

It strikes me, as I lie looking up at the stars that, if we abide by other people's standards, we become shadows of ourselves. Too often when I am with other people I hand over my freedom and values as if they are the price of admission to companionship. I expect others to be as harsh with me as the critic living in my mind—the critic with my mother's voice.

Discomfort moves over me like a breaking wave. My mother and I have not spoken in years. There was no single argument, or even a series of fights, that led to our estrangement. It was impossible to argue with her. She's never wrong.

When Babe arrived on the scene and insisted on changing

everything, the slim fissures that had been there all along began to widen. My mother clutched at me like a drowning person, except she didn't want to be saved—she wanted to pull me down with her. She ridiculed Babe and tried to suffocate her. She did not want a living daughter, she wanted the puppet I had been for too many years. When I tried to explain what Babe meant to me, she viciously attacked me; when I asked her to accept me for who I was or leave me alone, I didn't hear from her again.

Remorse flashes through me. It is difficult to be at odds with one's mother. At times it is more than difficult—it is devastating.

I peek over the edge of my bag. There's no sign of the dawn that will chase the stars from the sky. The feeling of elation I woke with evaporates like steam from a boiling kettle. After a few moments, I sigh and roll over, to stalk the thief that apprehended my sleep. My journey through the canyon may prove more of a trial internally than externally.

Morning touches the earth lightly, blending the sweet smell of tamarisks with water and sand. This scent is so distinctive

to the canyon that if I were to be taken to these shores blind-
folded after many years away, I would know instantly where
I was by the aroma that lingers here.

Lazily, I look down the steep bank toward *Sunshine Lady*
and bolt out of my sleeping bag. Forgetting the cold, which
raises goose flesh on my bare skin, I dash to her. Like a cat
stranded by a flood, she is perched precariously atop two
boulders. If I didn't know better, I'd think she climbed on
them deliberately to play a joke on me. Déjà vu hits as I
recall a friend pushing his rock-bound raft back into the
river early one morning. It took three strong men to move
the boat, but only one to repair the eighteen-inch tear in the
tube caused by sliding it over the knife-edged rocks it had
been stranded on. The recollection is strong enough to stop
me abruptly at the river's edge.

I'm not sure which concerns me more: the three strong
men needed to move the raft or the possibility of seriously
ripping *Sunshine Lady*. I approach her cautiously as if I'm
afraid of scaring her off her perch. I pat her bloated side to
reassure her, or myself, that the situation isn't as bad as it
appears. Fearing the worst, my fingertips reach underneath
her, examining the rock for sharp ridges. I withdraw my hand

and push gingerly against a tube. Much to my surprise, she slides easily down the side of the boulder, placing her more askew than she was before. Moving to the other side, I push again and with a loud slurp, she is floating.

I start a fire and cook breakfast. While I eat—potatoes fried to a golden brown, eggs scrambled with onions and cheese, an English muffin toasted over the fire with butter and jam and coffee brewed to perfection—I watch the sun grace the far side of the river. It's warm and inviting, and as remote and unobtainable as if it were on another planet. I pack up.

As soon as I reach the center of the river, the longed-for sunshine hits me, chasing away the last of the morning chill. I remove my sweater. During the summer months I'd be happy for the shade, now I wish there wasn't so much of it.

Sunshine Lady is caught by a strong current that takes us into a beguiling stretch of river called the Roaring Twenties. The canyon is spacious here, with straight walls rising up away from the river banks on top of talus slopes. The broadened river channel dashes around corners and over sudden drops, exploding with mirth and gaiety. Rapids, large and small, come close together, capriciously splashing and playing, deceiving with a laugh. They cajole me into relaxing, before springing a carefully hidden hole upon me, or tipping the raft on end.

Twenty-four-and-a-half Mile Rapid has a reputation. Bert Loper, the "old man of the river," died here in 1949, though speculation contends he succumbed to a heart attack and not to the rapid. He made his first traverse of Grand Canyon at the age of seventy and died just weeks before his eightieth birthday while rowing the river he loved.

At some water levels Twenty-four-and-a-half Mile Rapid can be surprisingly gentle. At other levels it is wicked. On my most recent trip I captained a paddle boat on a fun and easy run. I expect the same today and see no reason to scout. But as I approach, I begin to wonder if I'm in the right place. I pull into an eddy and walk along the shore to take a look.

I step on boulders of various shapes, sizes and colors strewn across the bank next to the river. Subtle shades of pinks, greens, browns and grays mix randomly like marbles in a sidewalk game. I move from one boulder to the next, only occasionally stepping down on the sand and brushing past the sharp-edged grass that grows between rocks. Tamarisk and willow trees hide the river from view. I keep going, stepping up, then down, over, across and up again. At the center of the rapid the trees thin enough to give me an unobstructed view. What I see startles me. The river is high. Much higher than I have ever seen it before. A small tremor moves through me as I study the powerful waves and holes that create more of a challenge than I bargained for. I scout carefully and head back to my boat.

Midway along the route, the drone of an engine breaks the silence. I look upriver expecting to see a large motor rig about to join me. Nothing is visible. The sound continues. Then almost directly overhead and close, much closer than the noise indicates, a small airplane glides fifty feet above my head. I stop walking and meet someone's eyes. I wonder if the Park Service is spying on me. Don't they know what solo means?

Confidently I take up the oars and pull toward the center of the river, wishing I could see around the bend that hides the rapid from view. It comes soon enough and when the entire rapid is spread out in front of me, my self-possession is replaced by panic. This rapid is totally different than the one I scouted. Did I place my mind on hold while standing on shore? What else can explain the alien whitewater? A cognizant voice reminds me I'm in the center of the river; the perspective is different. I quickly abandon my original plan, lean hard against the oars and row my boat stern first into the smaller of two holes. *Sunshine Lady* shudders from the impact, then continues through the rapid, heavy with several hundred pounds of water. I don't speculate on what might have happened if I'd turned over.

Twenty-five Mile Rapid is next. I stop to look at it, still shaking slightly from my encounter with Twenty-four-and-a-half Mile Rapid. It looks benign enough, hardly a rapid to have claimed the lives of some early explorers. But knowing rivers and rapids as well as I do, I can hardly blame Twenty-five Mile for exacting retribution on men who weren't wearing life jackets. It's well known Mother River doesn't like a smart aleck.

Halfway through the Roaring Twenties the canyon changes dramatically. Redwall Limestone rises abruptly out of the river. Although naturally light gray in color, the sheer walls are stained red by the Hermit and Supai Formations above. Polished by the unseen hand of nature, the walls emanate a radiance unmatched elsewhere, causing the Colorado River's first explorer, Major John Wesley Powell, to name the entire upper section of the river corridor Marble Canyon. Beaches are infrequent and sparse, and here and there small and sometimes large caves dot the Redwall. It is a massive formation, perhaps the most spectacular in the canyon, and entering it I feel as if I am shrinking in size.

The river calms, the Roaring Twenties no longer roar. The next moderately large rapid is more than twenty-five miles away. Time to relax, but as I travel past familiar places I grow apprehensive. Beaches I have previously stopped at for lunch, a cave opening I have explored, places I've camped are all considerably smaller. Buried under a flow I hadn't counted on, buried under more river than I might be able to handle. How much water will the Bureau of Reclamation let out of Glen Canyon Dam? The hair on my neck stands up.

I round a bend and see the translucent falls of Vasey's Paradise. A lush garden of verdant ferns, golden columbine, lobelia, crimson and yellow monkey flowers and poison ivy thrives beneath the waterfall. I pull into the eddy at the bottom of the falls, make a sandwich and linger, watching the water spurt out of a cave in the Redwall then fall freely through space, each drop sparkling in the sunlight like a ribbon of precious gems. After an interlude, I fill my jugs with the fresh water and leave.

A mile later I stop again at Redwall Cavern. Major Powell declared the cavern would seat fifty thousand people. Edward Abbey, a radical conservationist and wilderness writer, claims Powell was high by a digit. It's easy to exaggerate when you don't expect anyone to check up on you.

The cavern is wedge-shaped, like a clam with its shell opened at a forty-five-degree angle. I walk to the back until I can no longer stand upright. The sand under my bare feet is powdery and full of tiny mouse tracks. At the very rear of the cavern I kneel facing outward and experience the full expanse of the chamber. I run, raising a fine cloud of dust after me. I jump. I pace it off. I take photos, racing in front of the camera before the shutter goes off.

I stop. The cavern's ambiance tempts me to stay, to join prehistoric ancestors in the night as a fire throws giant shadows on the walls. The niggling voice of conscience reminds me that Redwall Cavern is off limits to campers. I hesitate. One person during the off season can't make much difference.

The light drone of an airplane breaks the silence and helps

make up my mind. I untie *Sunshine Lady* and push off. Redwall Cavern slips out of sight. I glance up. The plane is above the highest cliffs but is out of place against the gray sky and somber walls. Even at that distance it is an invasion of my privacy.

Touches of gold paint the uppermost cliffs of the canyon as I slide along on the placid, dark river toward a sandy beach two miles downstream at Nautiloid Canyon. I pull into the fast-moving eddy, crawl under the feathery branches of a tamarisk and tie *Sunshine Lady*'s stern line securely to the trunk.

Beyond the tamarisk trees, the beach opens up to a small camp that could comfortably accommodate eight to ten people. Footprints meander haphazardly around the beach, bringing the presence of other humans into my realm of solitude. I wonder how far ahead they are. Backed by a wall of Muav Limestone on one side and trees on two others, the site is sheltered and private. The fourth side slopes down to a wash that descends from the mouth of the side canyon. I suppress the urge to explore. By the time I find firewood and set up camp it is dark.

I finish dinner and return food items to the metal boxes

to discourage mice, skunks and ringtail cats from swiping a midnight snack. I lie on top of my sleeping bag, my hands encircling a hot cup of tea, and stare into orange flames that heat the cool air. When the fire burns down, I spread out the coals and watch them twinkle like city lights as seen from above until I nod into sleep.

I wake with an uneasy feeling that has kept me restless throughout the night. The first hint of dawn sketches patterns in the sky. I stride down the beach to my boat. A cool breeze nips at my bare legs still carrying the sleeping bag warmth around them. My toes knead the fine grains of sand with each step.

Earlier, while it was still pitch black, I awoke sensing something was wrong. I checked *Sunshine Lady*, concerned that the river, still rising when I went to bed, had impaled her on the trees. I cast the beam of my flashlight over her. The water level had dropped slightly from its high point and the stern line was taut. I considered loosening it in case the water dropped even more, but that would have required crawling under a tamarisk. With sleep still strong upon me, I decided to leave it alone. Now, with the clarity of hindsight, I wish I had taken those few extra moments. *Sunshine Lady* is completely beached. A boat-length of sand lies between the river's edge and her bow.

I walk entirely around her, then plop down on the edge of a tube. The obvious way to reunite my raft with the river is to unload her completely, drag her to the water and reload.

If I start now, I'll be on the river by noon.

I scowl at the thought and give the matter more consideration. There must be another way. Of course. Since I can't move the raft to the river, I'll let the river come to the raft. The water rose the previous evening; logically it will rise again this evening.

Sagacity escorts me to breakfast. After cleaning up, I follow the wash into the mouth of Nautiloid Canyon, named for the squidlike fossils embedded in its limestone floor. As with so many Grand Canyon hikes, this one is vertical. Without thinking about the difficulty, or my previous fears of the ascent, I climb twenty feet up the Muav Limestone, using small indentations in the rock as support. Then I scale a shorter, easier wall that takes me to the interior of the canyon. A strip of blue sky, two hundred feet overhead, is all that is visible above walls that narrow and curve inward. I poke around like a bug at the bottom of a vase.

I wander less than a hundred feet to the back of the cul-de-sac, around a few large boulders, then come out again and walk onto ledges that flank the mouth of the wash. Finding a flat rock in the sun, I sit down among the agave, hedgehog and barrel cacti. A tranquil river flows between perpendicular Redwall Limestone rising five hundred feet out of the water. Above the Redwall, the other layers rise even higher, dominating the river corridor.

Time passes slowly in this timeless land, giving me space and empty hours to think. The pace of life has slackened to a virtual standstill, imparting the sensation that life is infinite and it doesn't matter what I do, or if I do anything at all. I hold still, trying to remain as motionless as the plants and rocks around me. I want to absorb the placidity of the canyon's silence, allowing it to assuage the anxiety that courses through me. I have been forced to stop my perpetual motion, and the contrast to my usual existence of moving and doing and accomplishing is extraordinary.

There is nowhere to go, for beyond the beach and small side canyon sheer walls cut off the possibility of hiking in any direction. It is the ultimate in confinement, yet I feel less restricted here than I do in the outside world.

During my guiding years the clients frequently asked: "When are you going back to the *real* world?" I usually replied: *"This* is the *real* world." They didn't like my answer, and sometimes it caused a rift between us. It hit too close to a core truth that most, if not all, of us intuitively know: Living your life chained to a job you hate in order to buy heaps of possessions that mitigate your job stress but keep you tied to earning a steady income is not a *real* way to live.

I read somewhere that having a job you hate can shorten your life. I believe it. Rising every day to meet someone else's schedule, processing meaningless documents, interacting with people who share no common ground, exacts a tremendous toll. I've been there. I've had my spirit and soul sucked into oblivion by it. I've fallen into the depths of depression because of it.

During my river years I avoided material wealth and confinement by not wanting. I chose freedom over possessions and commitments. I was successful at it for a long time. But cars, even well maintained ones, have a habit of breaking down, clothes wear out, rent must be paid and food purchased. When the patches wore thin on my patchwork quilt lifestyle, I went back to the easiest thing I knew: Secretaryville.

As I walk into an office the first day on the job, the front door closes with the clang of a prison gate. How I manage to get that far is a mystery to me. Interviews leave me speechless and wringing with perspiration. They must think they're talking to a nitwit. Maybe in that context they are.

"Where do you hope to be in five years?" the prospective employer asks.

Exploring new rivers.

"What are your goals?"

Traveling the world, writing books, loving well.

"Why do you want this job?"

I don't.

Having the good sense not to verbalize the comebacks that flash through my mind, the silence grows heavy as I search for the expected response. What is it they want to hear? As chance would have it, I receive an offer from the least desirable job I applied for. In the face of rising debt, I accept—then sit at my kitchen table and cry.

Early in life I became a classic underachiever. In response to a society that favored boys over girls, that warned girls to stay away from danger, that forbade us to be physically strong or take risks, I stopped trying. I did not strive to do my best or distinguish myself. There was no point to it. It would have garnered displeasure rather than praise. I faded into the background, learning how to get by with passing grades, just good enough to keep me from bearing the humiliation of being left back. In a perverse way, I felt I beat the system. But I was simply fulfilling what was expected of the average girl. In high school many teachers, male ones especially, discouraged girls from contemplating college or pursuing a career. My mother was worse. Whether I expressed interest in acceptable female professions such as teaching or library science, or traditional male occupations such as zoology or law, her response was the same: "College will be a waste. You're just going to get married and have children."

After high school my parents sent me out to seek a low-level job that was repetitive and boring. That job led to another, then another, each one totally meaningless and well below my intelligence and ability. These jobs provided something to do while I waited for Mr. Right to come along so my life could begin. I hated the jobs and the lack of recognition. I railed against egocentric, autocratic employers who had no interest in treating me as a worthwhile human being.

Although many of them were truly sexist, it did not occur to me that I was asking them to treat me in a more valuable manner than I was treating myself.

When I finally did get a job I enjoyed, I excelled at it. My enthusiasm did not pass by unnoticed, and I was promoted from my desk job to sales rep. It was an enormous gamble on the manager's part because everyone else in the company considered women unqualified for outside sales. The only woman already on the team was loud, aggressive and spoke like a stevedore. I accepted the honor, then conveniently broke my leg in a skiing accident a month later, making it impossible to visit my accounts. My leg took more than nine months to heal: only after I had been moved back to my previous position. During the embarrassment of the demotion, I gained my first insight into the fear of being successful. Success suggested I was independent and therefore unfeminine. I would be undesirable to men; I would no longer be considered pretty or alluring. It was safer to break a leg.

I gaze upriver, my countenance shaken. I've grown a great deal since those days, but once again my life has reached an impasse. I don't want to repeat the mistakes of the past, but I don't know which way to turn. I remain frozen, afraid to move forward, to take risks. Doubt has replaced confidence. In order to regain the self-possession and courage I had when I left New York, I need to find Babe again. Hopefully I will, here on Mother River and Father Canyon where she was born.

I get up and walk around the rock peninsula, looking for a direct way down. A number of crevices begin with promise and end in a sheer drop of ten or fifteen feet. I abandon them and return to camp the same way I came up. The newly arrived sun has warmed my sheltered camp, and I shed my clothes and lie on my sleeping bag, book in hand.

A slight, hollow sound captures my attention. Blue-black feathers glisten in the sun as Raven observes my camp with a sharp, curious eye. She puffs out her neck, opens her mouth and makes a rattling sound, as if she's playing a percussion instrument. She gives two beats, stops, searches around for her non-existent band and repeats the rattle. Cocking her head one way, then another, she scrutinizes my camp, estimating how much she can usurp while I occupy the space. Tired of lying in one position, I move slightly. Unconcerned, she rattles again as if to prove it. Then, without warning, she flies off, wings audibly stirring the air, cawing raucously as if laughing at me.

I nap, burning my pearly backside in the process. Raven returns, strutting around my kitchen, inspecting bags, boxes, table and sand for food. When she pecks too hard at a bag, I yell. She disdainfully ignores me until I rise and run at her, waving my arms. Barely leaving the ground, she retreats to the perimeter of the camp, waiting for me to settle down so she might resume her activities.

The sun slides behind the rim, pulling a cool curtain of shade over the camp. I put on warm clothes and prepare dinner. After a day of idleness I am ready to begin moving again. I expect the water to rise and therefore go about my work with the conviction that I will be leaving camp in a short while. It does not occur to me that the river will not come up as high as it had the previous evening. Nor do I even question why I am so determined to leave camp that night. I have planted the idea firmly in my head and do not consider an alternative. Even when I check the river level and find that it hasn't moved from its low point, I'm only mildly surprised. I've made a plan and assume the river will cooperate. In order to be certain I am not imagining the river's inertia, I place a stick upright in the wet sand at the exact point where the river meets the shore, hoping the next time I look the water will have moved past the stick. Waiting for water to rise is like staring at the face of a clock in order to watch the passage of time.

Finally the river begins to creep up the bank. With a sense of assured satisfaction, I wash dishes and pack everything in its proper place. The rising water slows. I stare at it, willing it higher. I have finished tying and the river is still far from my raft. I look at the top of the canyon walls. They glow brightly in the late afternoon light. I have an hour and a half or two hours before dark. I sit on the floor of the raft and meditate. When I finish, I move to the rowing seat, look through one of my ammo boxes and grab a book.

I glance up periodically, still confident the river will rise in time for me to take off. I visualize being lifted up by the water as on a magic carpet and whisked away from the beach. If people were to come along I might appear fairly ridiculous sitting at the oars ready to row a dry-docked boat. There is no doubt that I would be hard-pressed to adequately explain my situation. I flush with embarrassment, picturing the puzzled looks on the faces of the imagined party as I declare that I am waiting for the river. No different really than waiting for a streetcar. Except streetcars do not run at the bottom of Grand Canyon, and lone women are not usually found waiting to row a raft away on the happenstance of rising water.

I look up at the walls again. They no longer blush with the glow of late afternoon sun. Although the possibility of the river sliding under the full length of my raft that night or any time in the near future is dim, I cling hopefully to my plan of reaching Buck Farm Canyon's steep beach, six miles downstream, before dark. The light fades and the river remains at the front tubes of the raft. The streetcar is not going to show. With an air of resignation, I remove my sleeping bag and pad from the raft and walk up the beach.

6

Timeless Land

Leave it as it is. You cannot improve on it. The ages have been at work on it, and man can only mar it.

— *Theodore Roosevelt*

I surrender myself to releasing the knots I had hoped would stay tied until the last day of the trip. Bowlines, half hitches and truckers resist my prying fingers. As each bag and box is freed, I lift it off the deck and place it on the sand next to the raft. When I finish, *Sunshine Lady* lies in a narrow passageway formed by a large pile of gear.

Disrobed except for frames, decks and spare oars, she's sure to be light enough to move. I march confidently to the bow, grab a D-ring and pull hard. She doesn't budge. I lean on the tubes, pushing with all my strength. Nothing. Doubt nibbles away at my confidence. What an ignominious way to end my solo trip—waiting for someone to come along and help me get unstuck.

I begin untying a knot that fastens the forward frame to the raft. I stop. The frames don't add that much weight to the raft. Of course! When the water dropped, it shaped the sand to the contour of the raft. I position myself under the bow and lift, edging it over the ridge of molded sand. With new hope and energy, I move to the stern of the boat and lift the rear tubes out of the mold. It's a beginning. Moving around the raft from one side to the other, I pull and push and lift and wiggle my one-hundred-fifty-pound gray whale across the fifteen feet of sand to the river. When the front tubes are floating, I lift the rear end and, with a surge of strength, push the entire boat into the river.

After a brief rest, I commence loading. One at a time I carry army surplus ammunition boxes over to the raft, thanking Uncle Sam for making such a quality product. These boxes, originally designed to house missiles, rockets and shells, keep my food dry. Originally olive drab, the boxes are painted pale gray with white lids. Hidden within is enough food for three month-long solo trips. Eggs, cheese, yogurt, powdered milk, cereal, noodles, potatoes, rice, cabbage, tomatoes, avocados, onions, lettuce, cashews, peanuts, raisins, sunflower seeds, peanut butter, jam, canned goods, English muffins, bread, tortillas, crackers, apples and oranges are kept cool and dry in the metal boxes. I could eat the entire contents right now.

The heavy supplies are on board and tied firmly in place. I look around at a beach still littered with gear. Two water jugs, a safety line, boat pump, three waterproof bags filled with clothing and sleeping gear, one stuff sack with available dry clothes, a firepan, solar shower, tarp, spare life jacket and three bailing buckets line up like soldiers waiting for orders. I issue the command and start tying. By the time I'm finished, every piece of gear has hoopie going through it, and there are no loose ends. At last I snap on my oars.

I lean against the rear of the raft. My stomach growls and my arms and back ache. The air is heavy and gray. I scan the beach and push off. *Sunshine Lady* flies up the eddy and enters the main current without my touching an oar. Raven caws and glides toward my deserted camp. The chambermaid coming in to clean up. I hope I haven't left anything for her to do.

I browse around my boat, munching on a breakfast of peanut butter and strawberry jam on whole-wheat bread, and read my maps. Only occasionally do I look up to see where the raft is headed. The current is strong but placid, enabling me to appreciate the comforts close at hand. Even *Sunshine Lady* seems happy to be moving once again.

I pass a small natural bridge above Thirty-six Mile Rapid, named "The Bridge of Sighs" by the Kolb brothers during their trip in the winter of 1911. They thought this region of the canyon "gloomy and prison-like" and named the bridge after one in Venice over which condemned prisoners walked from trial to the dungeon across the canal. The Kolb Brothers obviously had a difficult trip.

Periodically, I take up the oars and row, enjoying the fluid sweep of the motion. I've decided to do eighteen miles. I'll pass up hikes at Buck Farm, Saddle and Little Nankoweap Canyons. If I had more time, I wouldn't need a schedule. If I had forty-five or sixty days, I might be able to cover the entire Grand Canyon. Then again, I might need a lifetime.

I come upon the talus from test holes that were dug into the Redwall at a proposed dam site. One of the great crimes against the earth, humanity and other living creatures would have been committed if David Brower of the Sierra Club had not placed full-page ads in the *New York Times* and *Washington Post* in June 1966, stating: "Only You Can Save the Grand Canyon from Being Flooded—for Profit." Instead, the flood came in the form of protest from the public, resulting in a series of laws being enacted to save Grand Canyon from further development by dam builders.

Amen.

I hope. Although we live in an era of expanding environmental awareness, we also live at a time when a growing population has increased the demand for electricity and water. With particular irony, the Southwest, with little natural water available, has become a desirable place to live. It is dry, it is warm, it is sunny. One might think it is an ideal environment, and yet people coming from the eastern and midwestern cities to escape the snow and cold proceed to air-condition it to escape the heat. Or they come from California to get away from the crowds and pollution and debase the new area. Many desert dwellers waste water, because of ignorance, laziness or selfishness. Bright green lawns, deciduous trees and swimming pools abound, demanding water that is not naturally available. This extravagant use of water is shocking and the low cost encourages waste. As some communities have discovered, consumption can be drastically reduced by increasing the price of water, but few have taken this important step to conserve water.

The quickest answer to a shortage of water is to build a dam. This avoids the real issue of waste, and ignores the need for everyone to learn about conservation, an unpopular approach because it takes effort and sacrifice. Most often dams are pushed through by financiers and politicians who stand to increase their capital or enhance their influence by the inclusion of another dam in their territory. They are a dominant group of people who usually do not care about the damage incurred by their actions, and who frequently acquire public support by expounding upon the benefits, often imaginary, a dam will bring.

Behind most dams lies an irreplaceable wilderness, an area that can provide escape from the overcrowding, pollution and frantic pace of the city. The greatest losses incurred when damming a river are often subtle: the simple pleasures of floating downstream "the easy, natural way," as Huck Finn proclaimed; enjoying the serenity of throwing a fishing line into a quiet pool; picnicking next to the sound of water playing over rocks.

Although Grand Canyon has no dams within its environs at this time, it nevertheless shows the effects of having the giant plugs of Glen Canyon Dam at the upper end and Hoover Dam at the lower end. The river is no longer "too thin to plow, too thick to drink," as it was when Major Powell ran it. Now, the river is a deep green color, apparently due in part to algae and in part to the elimination of the one hundred forty million tons of silt that once scoured the canyon every year. Instead the silt settles out in Lake Powell, trapped there to extend the life of Hoover Dam, over three hundred miles downriver. One dam built to save another. Today the sediment in Grand Canyon has been reduced to an average of twenty million tons, not enough to replace beaches when a high water release washes them away.

Before the construction of Glen Canyon Dam, the river fluctuated with the seasons, frequently raging at one hundred thousand cubic feet per second (cfs) in the spring with the snow melt from the Rockies, before dropping throughout the year to winter lows. Although it is commonly thought that dams enable river runners to have a longer season on the water, it is interesting to note that many of the old-timers ran the Colorado during the winter months, when water is traditionally at its lowest flow. In addition, the elimination of annual spring floods upsets the natural cleansing effect of high water. Tamarisk trees, native to the Middle East, take over, choking out the indigenous vegetation; rapids are able to grow in size and difficulty; and various human scars that mar beaches are left to remain as a painful reminder that nature has been checked by humans from doing her proper job.

Glen Canyon Dam has had another dramatic impact upon the canyon with the change in water temperature. Before the dam was built, the river ranged between temperatures of forty degrees in winter and eighty degrees in midsummer. With the water being drawn two hundred feet below the surface of Lake Powell, it never sees the sun and enters the river channel at a chilly forty-five degrees—all year long. This drop in temperature has caused the extirpation of some of the native fish and increased the danger of running the river for humans. Hypothermia is a serious, life-threatening condition; a long swim in forty-five-degree water can result in death.

Lake Powell, created by Glen Canyon Dam, is the second largest man-made lake in the United States. It is one hundred eighty miles long with nine trillion gallons of water and eighteen hundred miles of shoreline. It receives hundreds of thousands of visitors annually who contribute to the reservoir's pollution with heavy metals and human waste. Fuel from motors dumps the equivalent of the Exxon Valdez oil spill into the lake every four years. As popular as the lake is, I somehow doubt that if it disappeared today it would be as sorely missed as Glen Canyon, the exquisite place that Lake Powell drowned. The loss of Glen Canyon is real, felt by the people who never had a chance to visit it, along with those who were fortunate enough to spend time between its sandstone walls before it disappeared.

If the Environmental Protection Agency had been in existence in 1956, when Glen Canyon Dam was authorized by Congress, it is doubtful the dam would have been approved. The government misled people, and only David Brower and a few environmentally focused people raised a cry of concern. Unfortunately, it wasn't enough to prevent the dam from being built.

Now, however, there is a glimmer of hope that the

Colorado River can be restored to a natural state. In November 1996, the Sierra Club Board of Directors voted unanimously to support an effort to drain Lake Powell. This initiative is supported by the Glen Canyon Institute, Friends of the Earth, International Rivers Network and the Earth Island Institute. New studies show that Powell reservoir loses approximately one million acre feet of water every year to evaporation—enough water to meet the demands of cities the size of Phoenix or Salt Lake City. Removing Glen Canyon Dam would improve riparian life in Grand Canyon and farther downstream at the Sea of Cortez estuary. It could also help avert a potential catastrophe to Arizona, Nevada, Southern California and Mexico if the dam cracked due to poor engineering, flood, landslide, earthquake or human intent. The cost is insignificant when compared to the damage the dam inflicts on the environment. Dismantling Glen Canyon Dam and draining Lake Powell is an endeavor worthy of serious consideration.

I turn my back on Marble Canyon Dam Site and glide along on a river that hides all trace of my presence. The miles pass by quickly. The river meanders past Royal Arches, Tatahatso and Hansbrough Points, President Harding Rapid and Triple Alcoves—names applied to cliff forms and water currents by man, hoping to gain some connection to the infinite, or perhaps once again prove his mastery over nature.

The sun beats down, seeping through to my bones and lulling me into a relaxed sleepiness. At Saddle Canyon I stop for lunch, planning to eat quickly and be on my way. But it's not a day to rush, and I find myself involuntarily slowing down. Hurrying is in direct contrast to the essence of the canyon.

Sunlight graces the east wall, causing it to radiate warmth, and feathery branches of tamarisks show off various shades of green and gold. Behind the sloping beach there is a spacious camp. Finishing my sandwich, I get up and wander around into various alcoves.

Suddenly, out of the corner of my eye, I see a human form hanging in a tree. I cry out, then peer at the object. A heavy wool sweater stretches across the branches of a tamarisk as if the owner had placed it there to dry after a wet day on the river. I wonder where the person is now. Gingerly I pick it up, ready to drop it if it should change into a ghost, and hold it up to myself. It's a little large for me but in good shape. I throw it over my arm and head back to my raft.

Two hours later I enter Nankoweap, a broad expanse of vistas, plateaus, side canyons and Anasazi granaries high in the cliff face. In a dramatic sweep of nature's hand, the right side of the canyon opens up. The escarpment stands back a mile from the river, and the North Rim is reduced to a hazy blue wall in the distance. Angular talus slopes lead up to the Redwall, high above river level, with mesquite, tamarisk, Mormon tea, cacti and other flora dotting the landscape. In contrast, the south bank's perpendicular walls rise five hundred feet almost directly out of the river.

The sun has long since departed. I play the boat along the edge of the current to the top of the long, shallow rapid around the Nankoweap drainage. I sweep both oars through the glassy current and catch a whiff of wood smoke. Holding the oars out of the water, I search the shoreline. Nothing. Not a telltale wisp of blue-gray; not a sign of another mortal being. My boat slides into the first small waves, and the smell of smoke hits me again. Am I soon to overtake the owner of the sweater? The phantom group could be at any one of three camps situated along Nankoweap's shoreline. I float uneasily into the rapid, hoping my imagination has conjured up the smoke. Part way through the rapid a beautiful lagoon, protected by a rock jetty on the upstream end, invites me in. I slide *Sunshine Lady* up to a sloping sand berth.

I sit for a moment waiting for the trepidation of meeting other people to subside, then take out a Henry Weinhart beer and lounge on a tube. Five days alone and I'm turning into an antisocial hermit. There's not a hint of loneliness, not a trace of fear—only harmony with the natural world, a spiritual bond with the canyon and the river that would be interrupted by other humans. I take a long pull on the thought and the beer.

I make my way along a narrow trail, fringed with dry, tawny grass, that leads to the Anasazi granaries. The path takes me through a forest of thorny mesquite trees, many of which are charred, ghostly reminders of a fire that swept the area years before. I pick one trail, then another, maintaining a general direction toward the granaries, though I cannot see above the tops of the trees. When the trees end abruptly at the base of a steep hill, I begin climbing a well-defined trail between boulders with needle-sharp surfaces and cacti with protruding inch-long thorns.

I stop often, examining plants and rocks, watching a lizard scurry out of my way, taking in the vista. A shining ribbon of water curves around sandbars and between walls that rise in tiers like the layers of a wedding cake. At the top of the rubble-strewn hill I can see for miles, and everything diminishes in size except the expanse itself, which grows larger. A broad plain, crisscrossed with animal trails, stretches out in front of me. I search the terrain carefully. Within that vast area there is no one else to be seen. The owner of the sweater is not around.

I turn away from the open vista and look up at the Anasazi granaries. The masonry structures sit at the top of the talus slope against the base of the Redwall on a shelf about five hundred feet above the river. The rose-buff color of the brick pueblos creates a camouflage, making them a natural hiding place. The Anasazi did not live in the rooms but used them to store their grain, grown on the silt bars below. Anasazi, "the ancient ones," built these structures about one thousand years ago. It is a difficult number to grasp. Juxtaposed against the age of the canyon it is no more than a few minutes' time; compared with my own forty-two years it is impossibly long.

The entrance to the structures is ten to fifteen feet away and requires a climb up a rock ledge. One slip and I'll fall into history as surely as the Anasazi have. I look up at the granaries again. Fear has always kept me from going beyond this point. On impulse I decide to risk it and look for a way up.

I reach the granaries easily and sit in front of them, looking out over the river and camps. It is a comfortable spot and less precarious than it appears from below. I look behind me and begin inspecting the series of tiny Anasazi rooms, recalling Colin Fletcher's similar examination in his book, *The Man Who Walked Through Time*. He housed himself in a "master cubicle" and fantasized an Anasazi constructing the dwelling carefully and patiently. I try to do the same, imagining the presence of people of another era. All I see is Colin Fletcher doing it.

At the outset of the climb a fleeting thought made me hesitate. Now it returns, bringing a rush of perception with it. With no one around to rescue me . . .

I am forced to be truly independent. I can't fake it in this vast solitude when my life hinges on how well I can take care of myself. At no other time or place in my life have I been as compelled to succeed on my own as I am here—alone in Grand Canyon. And in being faced with true independence I begin to see the bits and pieces of dependency that cling to me. The dependency of wanting to be rescued that goes far beyond the desire to have another person present in the event I hurt myself. I still carry the belief that being dependent is feminine and attractive. That's the catch. I want autonomy, but if I achieve it, I fear I'll be unlovable. I learned early in life to garner attention by being slightly helpless. Just now and then, here and there.

When I left New York, Babe dragging me all the way, I made a clean break with my old way of life, at least externally. I changed the things that represented my old image. I allowed my hair to grow back to its natural light brown color and felt a sense of relief to be rid of the false blond. I no longer dressed in a manner that provoked sexual attention. I was looking for a real person with her own voice, her own ideas, her own values.

A large part of that search involved living in a Lakota tipi. It was an experiment with a lifestyle and a statement that I didn't have to conform to societal expectations if they were not part of my individuality. At the risk of convincing everyone in a small town in western Colorado that I was crazy, I asked about places to pitch my unusual home. I wasn't making any progress until I met Jill, a woman dealing with her own demons of independence and femininity, who happened to own five hundred acres of ranch land backed up by a wilderness area. She offered me a sheltered spot, flat and private, ideal for my purpose. My retriever Amanda, along with the horses, goats, sheep and a wintering herd of elk with whom I shared the land, approved. My closest human neighbor, a man living half a mile away in a shelter that was three-quarters underground, with only the south face open to the sun for heat and light, welcomed me. I only hoped I could create as practical, comfortable and beautiful a home as he had.

My new home arrived via UPS from tipi makers in Oregon; I found lodgepoles in the National Forest. After an exhausting day raising the poles and fitting the canvas around them, I dug a small firepit, then covered the rest of the floor with straw and newspaper for insulation before placing rugs down for comfort and beauty. I made a bed frame that raised me a foot off the ground and used a foam pad for a mattress, covering it with sheets and blankets. I built shelves and placed them against the tipi liner for food and books. A rough-hewn table served as a desk. When all was ready, I sent out invitations to a housewarming during the Moon When The Ponies Shed.

In designing the tipi, the Plains Indians combined the practical with the aesthetic. Warm in winter and cool in summer, it provides shelter from rain, snow and the blazing sun. It is relatively easy to move. Its conical shape dots the prairie with symmetrical beauty. Whether painted with elaborate designs or plain, it stands with its back to the wind, its door open to the rising sun. Moon shadows dance across it at night, and a light from within makes it glow like a beacon in the desert. The smell of the earth after a rain, the sound of the wind, the song of a coyote all gracefully affect the dweller's existence. Like a bird in a nest, living within it is natural and potent. As Black Elk said, "There is no power in a square."

The cover, wrapped tightly around ten or more poles that pierce the sky many feet above the canvas, is a few inches off the ground. Inside, the liner's flap lies on the earth, covered with rugs. When a fire is built in the center of the floor, the rising hot air draws cool air upward from between the cover and liner, allowing the smoke to curl out the hole at the top.

During the sweltering days of summer, I rolled up both the liner and cover to allow breezes to waft through.

I had to master everything about this new lifestyle in the same way a child assimilates information when she is young. Babe was ecstatic; the old me was frightened out of her wits. Nothing could be taken for granted. Although I had already learned how to cook over an open fire and bake in a Dutch oven at whitewater school, having to do it every day as the only means to prepare meals gave it a new perspective. When I needed firewood, I watched the men at Jill's farm, who made cutting and splitting wood look easy. I asked questions, then went back to my site confident I would do just as well. I was determined to do it myself, though the chain saw scared me to death, the ax was unwieldy and each piece of wood seemed to jump off the block with a life of its own. I also had to learn how to get around in the dark without a light by feeling the ground with my feet, trim the wick on a kerosene lamp, keep fresh food from spoiling without refrigeration and use water from an irrigation ditch for everything from drinking to washing dishes. A little more than a year after moving out of Manhattan I was a mountain woman, and I felt as if I had just come home.

After the first couple of months I was confident and proud of my achievements. This is a piece of cake, I thought. Then disaster struck.

The hard physical labor entailed in my new lifestyle weakened and exhausted me. While rain poured down outside my canvas shelter, pain racked my lungs. Thinking I had a bad chest cold, I treated it with aspirin and rest. I recovered slightly, then relapsed. Five days later, further weakened by lack of food, I dragged myself to a doctor. "Pneumonia," he said, and prescribed penicillin. I was better in a couple of days, ready to meet the next challenge. It arrived swiftly.

In the dark of a very dark night, Amanda woke me crawling from her bed onto mine. I put my hand on her and was surprised when I touched wet fur. Then I heard the sound of running water, a sound so familiar I forgot I was in my tipi, not on the banks of a river. The only water nearby was the irrigation ditch and that didn't gurgle like a river. I reached for my flashlight and, when I turned it on, received the shock of my life. A river ran through my tipi. I was in the middle of a flash flood. It took a week to clean up the mess and move my tipi to higher ground.

I only expected to indulge my fantasy one summer. The

hard work, the disasters, finding bugs in my bed, mice steal-
ing food or a number of other hardships should have added
a touch of reality to my quixotic notions. But when autumn
appeared and painted leaves carpeted the ground, I was determined to see through a winter.

I moved a wood stove over the fire pit, added a couple of
wool blankets and a down comforter to the bed and bought
heavy duty winter boots. When snow fell, sometimes by the
foot, I skied out to my pickup truck and brought groceries
home in a backpack. To keep my body heat from escaping, I
mastered the art of changing clothes without stirring the air.
I slept warm, especially when Amanda turned the bed into a
one-dog night. Two-legged lovers were as scarce as snow-
flakes on a hot stove.

But I didn't care, for I was fiercely protective and proud
of my independence. I had learned to provide for my physical, financial and emotional needs without help from a man.
I had become a self-sustained unit. I cherished Babe and was
ashamed of the old me. I wanted to bury her, forget she ever
existed.

The *experiment* ran for four years, through days that ranged
from one hundred degrees to twenty below zero, three moves

and different climates. The tipi is gone now. The cover disintegrated from too much weather; the poles hold someone else's lodge erect. All I am left with is nostalgia. The memory of an uncomplicated lifestyle that was far richer than living in an air-conditioned condo with plush carpeting, a tiled bathroom and a dishwasher.

My hand grazes the cool, sandy earth, bringing me back to the present. Remembering the smoky odor of the tipi's canvas, the night sounds, the simplicity, creates a yearning in me that plucks at my heart like fingers on a mandolin. What's to prevent me from returning to that, I wonder.

"Not a thing," Babe declares. "When can we start?"

I chuckle and make my way back to camp.

The day passes in fits of laziness. Inertia is my biggest foe, and by evening only my growling stomach prompts me to lay aside my book and rise. Shattering nature's stillness with the clatter of metal pans against metal boxes, I begin dinner.

The ammo boxes, table, stove and firepan that make up my kitchen are less than twenty feet from *Sunshine Lady*. Her stern rests against the shoreline while her bow nods gently with the motion of the water. I drink in the peacefulness, wondering how it is possible that I am totally alone in this vast wilderness. I oil a Dutch oven and heat up charcoal briquettes for the specialty of the night—spinach lasagna—and realize with a start that I'm not alone after all.

A rock wren observes me quizzically from the refuge of the boulders that cover the jetty. Her brown and white body, five inches long from a thin beak to a broad tail, blends in among the rocks where she lives. She chirps and hops, chirps and hops, twisting her head one way, then another, as she surveys her surroundings. When she determines that she is safe, she flits from one rock to another, quickly and decisively, edging closer to the kitchen. I watch her, wondering what attracts her attention. It can't be my dinner. It has nothing substantial in it like bugs or worms. Then, with a whirring of wings, she flies to the boat, landing on an ammo box. She looks around as if she's testing the danger and reliability of this foreign object. Satisfied with its stability, she inspects the craft, darting from box to frame to tube to thwart until finally she disappears from view below deck. A moment later she reappears and flies back to the rock jetty. She remains on the rocks a few minutes, then returns to the raft, determination in every beat of her wings. *Sunshine Lady* is obviously this rock wren's idea of heaven. I visualize her accompanying me downriver, riding on my shoulder through rapids, nesting on my sleeping bag at night.

A subtle change in sound shifts my attention from the wren to the river. It is falling fast. I drop the parmesan cheese on the table and scramble around on the boulders, pulling the raft out to deeper water. I tie the bow and stern lines in different directions to keep *Sunshine Lady* stationary over a deep pool. Back in the kitchen I look around for the rock wren, but to my great disappointment she has disappeared.

I eat lasagna and garlic bread by candlelight, then lie in the sand by the fire. A waxing half moon fights for space with the clouds until it gives up and drops behind a ridge. An imposing wall across the river crowds closer in the darkness, leaning forward over my campfire like some great god of the night trying to warm himself. The vastness of the ebony sky and the immensity of the canyon grow larger, shrinking me in size. I hold a glorious feeling of solitude in my heart as I float weightless through the spaciousness of the canyons of the Grand and of my soul.

7

Fellow Travelers

I am tempted to write "my Canyon," so possessive can that place make one feel. But the Canyon is not mine, nor anyone's.
— *Edward Abbey, "In the Canyon" in* Outside *magazine*

A leaden sky and air tinged with autumn encourage me to remain in my sleeping bag. Coffee, chocolate, a book, that's all I require. I prod myself. It's time to move on again, to let the miles slip away under my raft.

I pull *Sunshine Lady* back to the sloping beach. The rock wren zooms between the beach and the raft, only taking refuge in the rocks when I come too close. Her chirps are high pitched and frantic, scolding me for moving *Sunshine Lady* and entreating me to remain at camp. "I'm sorry little lady, but I can't stay. The river calls me downstream." She chirps, distress obvious in the small peep.

I make breakfast and pack, humming softly to myself as I put things away and tie gear on the raft, enjoying the quiet of an early morning. I change from camp clothes into river clothes, scan the beach for forgotten items, and coil up the stern line. I push gently against the raft, then stop abruptly when the eddy tosses me a bombshell. A raft carrying two men floats into my harbor. *What are you doing in my canyon?* The words reverberate in my head.

I shift awkwardly from one foot to another, like a schoolgirl caught cheating on a final exam. An impulse to run and hide pumps me full of adrenalin. But they've seen me already and there's nowhere to go, a fragment of logic interjects. *Besides, how can I hide a fifteen-foot boat?* I crumble onto the tube of my raft and wait.

Blue jeans, a plaid shirt and an orange life jacket adorn the invader at the oars. A thatch of blond hair escapes from beneath the sweatband of a cowboy hat. Not your standard Grand Canyon garb. The passenger is bundled against a winter's day of rafting in the Arctic, making it doubtful his life jacket could keep him afloat. He holds a fishing pole over the water and his complete absorption in it does not waver for a moment. They seem intent on making contact but neither has acknowledged me. Maybe I'm invisible. I hope I'm invisible.

The cowboy stops rowing when he's five feet away. "Howdy," he says. I'd be less surprised if he had ridden up on a horse.

"Hello."

We stare at each other. His blue eyes are friendly. I can almost hear the desperate search for words going on in his mind. The fisherman ignores me.

"Has the rest of your party gone ahead?" he asks.

"No."

Puzzlement chases the congenial look away. "Are they upriver?"

"No." It's not the answer he expects. "I'm alone."

His eyebrows lift very slightly. I can't tell if he's surprised or just nervous about being in the company of a lunatic. "How many days have you been out?"

I think for a moment. "This is my seventh day." It's the only number I can remember. I lost the date and day of the week upriver somewhere.

"You're the first people I've seen since I started." I stumble over my words in the unfamiliar use of language. "It's quite a shock," I add as explanation for my unpolished speech.

He takes no notice. "I'm Pete," he volunteers, "from Idaho. We put in three days ago." Leaning his forearms on the oars, he waits for me to respond.

"My name is Patch." I smile at him. The silence grows large between us. I open my mouth to ask if he and the fisherman are traveling alone, when three boats carrying five people float into the far edge of the eddy. The boatmen hold the boats in place with a slight sculling of oars.

Pete ignores them, and the fisherman is still engrossed in his rod and line.

"You should have joined us last night. We had a great fish fry." His voice raises with enthusiasm. "In fact, I'm surprised you didn't hear us. We made a hell of a racket."

"Where were you camped?"

"On the other side of this pile of rocks," he waves his arm toward the jetty.

My hand flies up to my mouth, the fingers twist the edge of my lip. In my absolute solitude I was only a hundred yards from them. "I didn't hear a thing." I wonder how that was possible.

Pete pulls slowly on his oars, heading toward the waiting boats. "You can join us tonight, if you'd like," he offers slowly. He hesitates. "It might be nice to run the Gorge with someone else."

Yes, the Gorge, I think. Only twenty-four miles downstream with some of the largest rapids on the Colorado. The first real test of my rowing skills and ability to cope with fear.

"Thanks. I'll think about it." I intertwine the stern line through my fingers. "I've really gotten into being alone," I add as an excuse, in case I don't show up.

I wait while the cowboy rows away, then pull the wool hat off my head and tuck it in a box. The rest of the group circles at the end of the eddy talking among themselves. I feel scrutinized and invisible at the same time.

I expect them to leave, but a moment later another boat slowly heads my way, with a lone oarsman. "Damn," I mutter under my breath and drop my gaze.

When the boat is a few feet away, I meet the blue eyes of a woman sitting comfortably at the oars of a boat a few feet longer than my Pro. She is larger than I am, probably about five-feet-nine or ten inches tall, with a medium build. Dressed in shorts, sneakers and a light sweater under her life jacket, she seems oblivious to the cool morning air. Wisps of blond hair stick out from under a cap, and her eyes dance with excitement.

"Hi, I'm Lynn. I couldn't be sure from the distance if you were a woman," she began. "Not too many women have done the Colorado alone. In fact, I know of only one—Georgie Clark."

Georgie Clark made her first run of the canyon by swimming the lower portion of it with a friend in 1945 and 1946. After that she bought an army surplus ten-man raft and began taking it down the river, sometimes alone. She was fascinated with the river and canyon and wanted to learn to run it well enough to take passengers. On these trips in her small boat she often deflated her raft and carried it around rapids or lined it through the rapid from shore. Both operations were hard work, especially alone, but often when she ran a rapid she would capsize. Although she rafted during the period before Glen Canyon Dam was built and therefore did not have to contend with the cold water, flipping proved to be as exhausting as portaging or lining. Finally, she tied three rafts together, mounted a motor on them and began offering trips to the general public.

"It's good to see women rowing the canyon," Lynn continues. "There are so few of us. I'm trying to get a job with this company," she motions toward the others, "but they're against hiring women." She states it as a fact, without bitterness. "We're deadheading to Phantom Ranch to pick up a group of passengers, but it's a training trip for me. They want to see if I'm able to handle the boat well enough to take clients in the future."

I nod, empathizing with her. "I've tried to get hired myself but have had no luck."

She smiles in sympathy. "I've often thought of running the Green River alone but have never done it. Now maybe I will." She looks around. "I'd better go. The others are waiting. I hope you'll camp with us tonight or at least stop for lunch at the Little Colorado." Her invitation is warm and genuine.

"Maybe I will," I call to her.

Without hesitation they take off. By the time I reach the main current they are out of sight, leaving me with a solitude that no longer feels comfortable.

I did fine alone the first six days but now that I've met these six men and one woman I'm consumed by an urgent need to join them. I row hard to catch up with the group and inwardly rage and rant for not maintaining my own pace. The harder I row, the more unsettled I become, yet I seem to have no control over my actions. This is not what I had envisioned if I met other people. I thought it would be a simple matter of saying hello, then waving goodbye.

I approach Kwagunt Rapid. Still no sign of the other boats. Suddenly this straightforward little rapid grows in size and importance, and I fear that each wave will capsize my raft.

At the bottom of the rapid I catch sight of the other rafts in the distance and relax my pace. We are spread out along the river so that each boat is a small, distant speck to the others. I'm still alone but the one-on-one relationship with the canyon and river is gone.

I draw in a large breath and let it out with a whoosh. My anxiety meter shoots up as it registers a need for guidance and approval, a yearning to accommodate and entertain, to show these seven strangers how brave and independent I am. Since they're mostly men, I also need to show my feminine side. In the few moments since they entered my space, I'm

ready to throw away my independence and question my personal belief system—as if their approval will validate my actions. The self-assurance that was mine the first six days on
the river vanishes like the delicate petals of a flower under a
strong wind.

Five miles below Kwagunt Rapid the canyon of the Little
Colorado River joins the main Colorado; I row *Sunshine
Lady* toward the confluence. I tie the raft where translucent,
turquoise water mingles with the dark green of the main
Colorado. The other boats are not in sight. I grab a few lunch
items out of a box and walk along sandstone ledges, around
a corner and into the side canyon. Four boats are tied along
the shoreline of the smaller river. Feeling shy, I walk over to
join the group.

Names, pieces of melon, cookies and laughter are passed
around as introductory offerings. The atmosphere is tinged
with a competitive friendliness as we share stories about rivers, feeling each other out, questioning one another's exper-
tise in an oblique manner. No one asks about my trip and
there is no reference to it, as if I have a handicap no one
wants to acknowledge.

I look at Lynn, hoping for a continuation of the affinity

we shared that morning, but her attention is centered on one man and she no longer has time for me. I have the strong impression that our personal connection must remain private. How often have I been in this same situation? Women's thoughts and feelings and talk are minimized because they do not fit into a male society. Where does that leave us if we want to become professional boatwomen on the Colorado? Do we have to give up our femininity? There are women who seem able to balance the two sides. They maintain their identity as women and row heavy boats through big water. But they are less than ten percent of the guiding population. How many women will be allowed to join the ranks before the number intimidates the entrenched male community? How many new boatwomen will those women who are already established as guides allow to join their ranks? Too often jealousy keeps women from helping each other gain access to what has been a male-dominated arena.

These men are nice but seem uncomfortable with me. Is it my own shyness, my inability to join a group and talk freely that makes them uncomfortable—or the fact that my solo trip makes a statement that I am capable of living and doing and being without a man?

I'm drowsy from too much lunch and sunshine when John looks at his watch. "It's time to go," he announces. "We've got a lot of miles to make before camp."

The others rise, gather up the few things on shore, and get on their rafts. Pete looks at me. "Are you coming?"

It's the opportune time to say goodbye. "No" forms on my lips, but "yes" escapes. Apprehension about running Hance Rapid and the Inner Gorge alone, and the fear that if I don't join them, they will think I dislike them, drives me to agree to something I don't want and don't need.

Shortly after the Little Colorado, the river's general direction changes from south to west. Fault lines slice through the formations on either side of the river, a black lava flow covers the Tapeats Sandstone and the deep red of the Dox Formation dominates at river level. It is here that Major Powell wrote his stirring words:

> *We are now ready to start on our way down the Great Unknown. Our boats, tied to a common stake, chafe each other as they are tossed by the fretful river. . . . We have an unknown distance yet to run, an unknown river to explore. . . . With some eagerness and some anxiety and some misgiving we enter the canyon below and are carried along by the swift water through walls which rise from its very edge.*

With effort I maintain the same pace as the other four boats, and by late afternoon we have gone ten miles since lunch. I pull over to a tiny beach for a short, necessary pee break and wave at Pete as he passes. I scan the small beach. A perfect camp for a group of one. I gaze at the river. They're out of sight and there's no way to let them know I'm not following. Would they worry, or even wonder what has happened to me if I don't show up? Would they think I'm rude or unfriendly, or worse yet, crazy?

I push off. The perfect opportunity to stop is thwarted by the need to conceal my eccentricity.

I run Unkar Rapid alone, staying away from the large hole on the left wall, riding easily through the long series of small waves. As I arrive within sight of Nevills' Rapid I catch up to the four boats getting ready to make the run. The last boat waits for me. The boatman yells, "We're camping at the beach on river left. You have to start pulling over before the end of the rapid."

I nod.

The light grows dim as I follow the other boats into camp. We have covered twenty-three miles, my longest day on the river since beginning the trip. I set up my tent, then join

Pete and three others by the campfire. Lynn and two men make dinner. The talk lingers over river experiences and mutual people we know. It's a familiar scene, and though I have enjoyed it in the past, I'm not entirely comfortable with it tonight.

Thick, black clouds migrate upstream while a fierce wind blows like a harbinger foretelling doom. The impending storm turns the canyon's mood dark and threatening. I crawl out of my tent and grab it as the wind blasts it off the ground, then collapse it and fold it up. I secure my few possessions on my boat and tie up the stern line. Pete and I are first at the oars, rowing our rafts against the wind-whipped waves to the middle of the river. A fine spray of water mists over me.

Less than a mile downstream we pull our boats into an eddy at the top of Hance Rapid and tie them securely to a tree. Without a word, Pete walks downstream to scout the rapid.

I fuss at the hoopie, tuck a couple of things away and throw on another sweater, which doesn't relieve the shiver traveling the length of my spine. The rest of the group arrives and immediately takes off to scout. They are out of sight when I finally jump off my raft. I follow them down the trail, cross Red Canyon's dry wash and climb a sand dune overlooking the rapid. On my way up I meet Pete and the fisherman heading back to their boat.

Like a number of rapids in the canyon, Hance is named after one of the early pioneers in the area. In 1884 John Hance became the canyon's first white settler when he built a cabin on the South Rim. During the ensuing years he ran a tourist business, constructed Old Hance and Red Canyon trails from the South Rim to the river, opened an asbestos mine and told a lot of tall tales.

Surveying the rapid, my stomach churns itself into a tight knot. This time my anxiety is justified. Hance Rapid is a massive boulder garden with unrunnable holes and rocks jutting above the foam. One of the three largest rapids on the river, it is the first of the trilogy that includes Crystal and Lava Falls. On the rating scale Hance is usually a ten and never goes below an eight.

I stand on the sand dune with Lynn and four of the men, watching Pete as he maneuvers his boat across flat water from left to right, descending down a relatively smooth channel in the middle of the river. I expect some discussion, but when he reaches the end of the rapid the others depart. I vacillate, look over the possible runs and return to my raft. Halfway back, the other boats pull away from shore. One by one they disappear downriver. So much for keeping up with them yesterday so I don't have to run Hance alone today.

I concentrate on the route I've chosen and push past giant holes, around rocks and over waves. By the end of the rapid *Sunshine Lady* resembles a pregnant whale with her floor stretched out by the weight of gallons of water. I'm soaked and can barely move the raft. I pick up a bucket and bail. It begins to rain heavily.

As the tail waves of Hance Rapid subside, the Inner Gorge begins, abruptly rising one thousand feet out of the river like the gates to the devil's corridor. Glistening black Vishnu Schist, the oldest rock in the canyon, interlaced with pink veins of Zoroaster Granite creates a tight inner chasm. A billion years of wind, water and silt have polished and molded these metamorphic rocks into sensuous shapes and gleaming spires. A provocative and dramatic beauty, with timeless rocks turning black and ominous under threatening skies.

The canyon is narrower than before. Hard rock resists

erosion and means big rapids, and some of those in the inner granite gorge are enormous. The river is in turmoil, breathing heavily like a runner after a marathon, flinging herself up in a mad, frenzied attempt to break out of her confines. Between rapids, she swirls and churns, sucking at the inflated tubes of a boat or spinning off into strong eddies that grasp a raft and hurl it back upstream.

A mile below Hance I catch up with the others. We row within sight of one another and occasionally come close enough to carry on a conversation. We run Sockdolager and Grapevine Rapids. The rain lets up. Half a mile above Phantom Ranch, I pull into an eddy and wave goodbye.

Phantom Ranch is the only human habitation in Grand Canyon. Stone and wood buildings are set a half-mile back from the Colorado River along Bright Angel Creek. This naturally tranquil place was selected in 1903 by David Rust, one of Grand Canyon's early settlers, as a camp for tourists and hunting parties. Ten years later it became known as Roosevelt's Camp after Teddy stayed there, and was changed to its current name in 1922 by Mary Colter, a visionary architect who was responsible for the construction of Phantom Ranch, along with a number of structures on the South Rim.

I amble past Phantom Ranch's center—ranger station, mule corral, dining hall and small cottages reserved for guests. Cottonwood trees tower in the side canyon, their massive branches reaching over cottages, pathway and creek. The sun makes a feeble attempt to penetrate the still-thick clouds.

The well-worn path takes me to the canteen, nestled at the far end of the ranch buildings. I smile at the woman behind a sliding glass door. She opens it. I order a cup of tea and a sandwich, and ask to look over the mail being held for river runners. She hands me a large stack of envelopes. I flip through them, extract half a dozen, then settle on a rock to read mail and eat lunch.

Before I've finished the first letter, the wind explodes through the side canyon, swirling dust, twigs and leaves everywhere. Cottonwoods thrash and bend, slamming branches to the ground. I dash inside the women's room and as my eyes adjust to the dim light I come face to face with another person. I stop short and peer at her—short, windblown hair, scarf tied casually around her neck. Beneath the weathered appearance there is a light in her eyes, a gleam of happiness and self-worth that is engaging. I start to say hello, then realize I'm looking in a mirror. I laugh at the absurdity of not recognizing myself and proceed to scrutinize my reflection. The woman in the mirror is strong and sure, warming me internally and giving me a glimpse of Babe.

I read my mail and write out a dozen postcards, covering the blank spaces with words of excitement and love. When finished, I leave my dark corner, mail the cards and discover a few more letters have arrived with the afternoon mule train. I devour them.

Wind and plump drops of rain accompany me the mile and a half to my raft. Cremation Camp lies across the river, a pocket of sand and rocks and tamarisks tucked between sheer walls of schist and granite. I slip on my life jacket and take up the oars. The eddy at the base of Cremation Camp is large. Still, there are numerous ways I could miss it. The thought wants to linger but I can't consider it. The next camp is miles downriver. I row *Sunshine Lady* to the extreme top of the near eddy, set my angle, then pull like hell across the current. At the last moment, I catch the far eddy.

I grab the tent bag, remove the poles and fit them together. Once the poles are erect, I lay out the tent and attach it hurriedly, then toss the rain fly over the ensemble, missing it as a gust of wind whips the fabric into the air. Lines tangle and the freestanding tent lifts with another gust of wind. I run and fumble and swear until the tent is firmly staked down.

The rain intensifies, soaking me to the skin. I return to the raft, untie my personal bags, throw them inside the tent and crawl into an interior that resembles a wet sand box. I sit inside the door and wonder how I can possibly enjoy camping.

I select the driest, cleanest spot on the floor and spread out my Therm-A-Rest and sleeping bag. Shivering like a shipwrecked sailor on the North Sea, I search through the bags for my warmest dry clothes. I slip on long underwear, turtleneck, wool sweater and wool pants.

The rain lets up and I crawl outside to look around, surveying the terrain for possible rock slides or flash floods. This small break in the otherwise impregnable schist is peppered with large boulders, interspersed with alcoves of flat, sandy spots. I look over a wash coming off the schist and follow the logical path a flash flood would take, tracing it down through rocks and sand to the river. My tent appears to be well out of the way.

As darkness descends, I return to my tent. I build a small shelter for a one-burner stove just outside the doorway, place a small pot of water directly over the burner and balance another pot containing leftovers on top of the first pot. When I hear the water boiling I reach over to turn off the stove. With a slight flick of my wrist, I catch the pot handle and knock the entire apparatus over. Salvaging a little food, I watch the water run away. The stove is full of sand and useless for the moment. My mood turns as gloomy as the weather outside.

I zip up the tent door and take out my journal. The page remains blank. Laying paper and pen aside, I open a book and reread the same paragraph again and again without absorbing a word. I turn out the light and listen to the sounds of wind and rain, wondering where Lynn and Pete and the others are.

A tear slides down my cheek. I spent the past two days wishing for solitude, and now that I have it I feel alone and vulnerable. Somewhere in the rain I lost that strong woman in the mirror. Instead, I'm scattered like dry autumn leaves in a wind, unsure of who I am and what strengths I actually possess.

~~~

I unzip the door of my tent. Fresh, clean air rushes inside, knocking me over with its purity. It slaps me in the face with invigorating suddenness, dives into my lungs and fills me with joy. Instantly I'm awake, ready to plunge into the day. A brilliant sky caps the earth with a fathomless blue. Not a particle of dust remains in the air, not a trace of a dark cloud.

It's the perfect opportunity to spread last night's damp clothes over rocks and hang them from trees. My sleeping bag and liner, Therm-A-Rest and the contents of my black bags follow. I haven't missed a thing. Almost. I cast off my clothes. The sun wraps its warm, gentle rays around me.

I clean my stove and, with greater care than I showed the night before, heat up water for tea and oatmeal.

When everything is thoroughly dry and fragrant with sunshine and canyon breezes, I begin to pack. My fingers concentrate on knots they know without help from my brain, which is useful since my mind is lost in the swirling currents that head directly for Horn Creek Rapid.

At low water Satan pops out at Horn with an ungodly cauldron of sharp rocks and huge holes. My initiation to this demon came one time when Dee's twenty-two-foot snout boat barreled into a jagged piece of schist that splintered the wooden splashboard and doubled the boat in half. Now, as I ride the fast current under Bright Angel Bridge, past Pipe Creek and Bright Angel Trail, scenes of that horrendous run replay over and over in my mind. I wave at hikers and watch mules send dust clouds to the rim. No amount of distraction releases the tension that tightens muscles in my shoulders and back. Fifty yards above Horn Creek Rapid I tie *Sunshine Lady* to a tree, test the line and walk on trembling legs to the brink of the rapid.

To my delight, a full-bodied river with glassy tongue and evenly spaced waves has drowned the dervish. Relaxed and confident, I sway with the roller coaster swells. I note a ray of sunshine streaming onto the river downstream and click a mental photo. Complacency is about to tear a yawn out of me when a hidden current grabs the raft and hurls her toward a solid pillar of schist. My left oar is torn from my grasp. I wait for the collision, but the raft stops before impact. I look for the fiend beneath the foaming boil that holds us a hair's width from the wall.

Fear rattles my teeth as I sit motionless on my seat. An impetuous move could cause the raft to flip—or worse—wrap against the wall, pinning me underwater. I pull cautiously on the left oar. Slowly, *Sunshine Lady* swings out. I have it licked. Another pull and the bubble will release us. I'm sure of it, until the current catches her stern and sucks the tubes under water. I leap away from the onrushing river to balance the raft, then reach out again with the left oar and swing the raft away from the wall. I stand in waist deep water and shake my head. "Okay, so I was a bit cocky. You didn't have to get so riled up about it."

Father Canyon chuckles, "Gotcha!"

I set a leisurely pace, savoring my solitude as I slip past glistening walls to Granite Camp. In the stillness of the hour before the earth turns its back on the sun and enters twilight, I unload my boat, gather firewood and pitch my tent. Then, taking my camera, I follow a path through the tamarisk trees, enjoying the sensual pleasure of a late afternoon glowing with long, slanting, golden rays. While morning light whispers blue, late afternoon light murmurs red and warmth, even in winter.

Emerging from the tamarisks I walk to the river's edge, take some photos, then climb twenty feet to the top of a large sand dune. When I reach the crest I am startled to see a man standing beside a tent, a camera pressed against his face.

He looks up.

"Hello," I call out, wishing I had escaped before he spotted me. As he returns my greeting, a blond head pops out of the tent, and a woman looks up at me.

We talk easily about the canyon, the weather and their travels around the world from their Australian homeland. Within a short time it is apparent we are kindred spirits, and later, when they join me at my campfire, we continue talking for hours about everything from politics to hiking. When the evening comes to a close, I'm sorry to see them depart.

As I settle into my sleeping bag, I realize how important it is to find kin—family bound not by blood and genes but by mutual love and support. The family I was born into is less mine than these people from another continent.

8

Whitewater

Then he rolled a river into the gorge, a mad, raging stream that should engulf any that might attempt to enter thereby.

— *Southern Paiute Legend*

The canyon is alive with creatures: lizards, scorpions, rattlesnakes, deer, coyotes, bighorn sheep, ringtail cats, skunks and mice. Most I'll never see, some will leave only their tracks and some, like the two quivering gray-brown mice trapped at the bottom of a five-gallon bucket this morning, plead with huge eyes for mercy. Bewildered by their predicament and terrified by my presence, the mice press tightly against each other, head to tail, as if by the sheer force of compressing themselves together they can vanish. "This is what curiosity will get you," I advise them. "In the future stay away from buckets. Next time you might fall into soapy dishwater and drown." Their quivering intensifies. I carry the bucket away from the kitchen and turn it on its side. Two gray streaks disappear into a tangle of tamarisk roots.

I return to the kitchen aware that the trip is changing once again. Today's energy is different from yesterday's. It's a subtle yet strong perception, like knowing someone is watching you before you actually see them. I'll be alone again. My solitary passage won't be interrupted. I welcome it. It's time to get on with my solo trip.

Solitude's biggest physical challenge commences at my doorstep in rapids that come one right after another. Big, difficult, scary rapids. From Granite, whose rumble I can hear from camp, to Hermit, one-and-a-half miles downstream, through Boucher, Crystal, the Jewels—Agate, Sapphire, Turquoise, Ruby—and others before and after them. Combined, they form the most difficult obstacle of my trip: more than eleven chances to mess up, to flip, to be thrown out of my boat or to succeed and feel wonderful.

The Colorado is a typical desert river with a negligible gradient that drops eight feet per mile through the length of

Grand Canyon, yet it contains some of the biggest rapids in North America. Unlike the steep gradient of mountain rivers, where water crashes through a narrow passageway over and around rocks creating a technical obstacle course, the Colorado heaves itself into towering waves or powerful hydraulics that form holes, reversals, boils, whirlpools and turbulent eddy fences. Voluminous amounts of water course through the bottom of the canyon. While mountain streams often flow at one or two thousand cubic feet per second, the Colorado River is considered low at levels below ten thousand cfs. As volume grows so does velocity and power.

Between each big drop, the Colorado River pools out, sometimes for less than a mile, more frequently for a distance of two to five miles and occasionally for more than twenty miles. The topography of the canyon determines where rapids occur. Adjacent to every drop on the Colorado lies the inevitable side canyon. A build-up of cumulus clouds over a particular drainage sends a heavy rainfall down a dry wash, turning it into a raging turmoil. As a flash flood gains momentum, rocks and boulders are spewed into the river, forcing it into a narrower space. If the flash flood is small, an inconsequential riffle is formed. But when a major storm drives huge boulders and tons of mud down a side drainage into the river, a rapid is born.

For many years, whitewater was considered unrunnable. During his trips of 1869 and 1872, Major Powell portaged or lined his boats around most of the canyon's big drops. He was an explorer and a scientist, not a whitewater boatman. But as time passed and interest grew, river runners developed techniques for navigating rapids, and a new sport was born.

A myth existed for many years, and lingers still, that maintains it takes a large, powerful man to row a boat through whitewater. The truth is, it takes brains to run a rapid—not brawn. The key to a flawless run is understanding the dynamics of a river. The direction and velocity of the current, the power of a hydraulic and the force of a cresting wave deliver specific messages to be read and examined closely, like important documents. I take it seriously. This chronicle could save my life.

Learning to maneuver a boat was a challenge, full of mistakes and triumphs. But when my heavy oars finally felt light, when my awkward strokes evolved into fluid motion and when I learned to read the complex language of a rapid, I gave myself a gift of exhilaration and vitality that transcended ordinary experience. And for every year I row, the joy of running rivers increases.

I walk along the narrow pathways that meander between the tamarisks to scout Granite Rapid. At the mouth of Monument Creek the jungle of feathery branches ends, cut off as abruptly as a sharp knife cuts off the head of a fish. The massive boulder garden that once barreled down the side canyon wiped out the trees. I step carefully over the boulders looking for a good vantage point.

A boulder garden on the left pushes most of the current to the right against a sheer wall, resulting in ten-foot curling waves that rebound off the wall at a forty-five-degree angle to the main current. Meanwhile, other curlers angle off the first, creating an upside down V. It's an ugly hydraulic, for it's often difficult, if not impossible, to keep a boat from turning sideways to one or another of the waves. As a result, runs through Granite are often wildly out of control. And there's no easy way to avoid the right run, for the left passage is blocked by two unrunnable holes, one at the top of the rapid and the other in the center.

I like holes as much as a cat likes a bath. They're dangerous and unpredictable. From exploding monsters that curl back upstream to quiet "keepers" filled with white, foaming, aerated water, holes always pose a problem. When water pours over a rock that is fairly close to the surface, it dives to the bottom of the river leaving a "hole" that must be filled in. The filling takes place when the surface of the river reverses itself into a backflow. Rowing a raft into a hole is akin to riding a bicycle at high speed into a pothole.

If a rock is very close to the surface or partially exposed, the hole behind it appears flat as water rushes back upstream toward the rock. The hole is called a "keeper" when it stops a raft cold and holds it in the bubbling froth where the backwash meets the downstream rush of water. I've had intimate rendezvous with keeper holes, and they've all been terrifying.

When a raft slips over the brink into one of these killers, it is pounded, spun around and shaken. Gear can be ripped off the raft, a frame bent, a seat snapped in two. During frantic seconds that seem like hours, as you try to keep the raft from flipping and from falling in the hole yourself, you search for a downstream current to grab with an oar in order to pull the boat out of the hole's grasp. If the hole is large enough, the downstream current is far out of reach and you remain stuck, looking into the face of death while recirculating around the hole until it decides to release you—usually after the raft is full of water.

It's easy enough to keep away from Granite's holes. The challenge lies in staying upright in the V-waves and missing a large swirling eddy at the bottom right of the rapid. The force of the water going downstream against the surge of the water traveling upstream forms the eddy fence, a fluvial barrier sometimes strong enough to flip a raft. Many, such as the one at the bottom of Granite Rapid, are powerful enough to make it extremely difficult, if not impossible, to cross in order to rejoin the main current.

I scout large rapids, reading them from the bottom up. I note each obstacle, its location and relationship to the main current. I have to: Once I start my run I'm committed, and if a hole or rock is in my path, I might need to take strokes away from it long before I actually reach it.

I push off from shore and pull hard on the oars, using my entire body to row the boat across the width of the river. My race with the current is a close one, and at the last moment I slip to the right of the hole and drop over the lip into the rapid. I point *Sunshine Lady*'s bow into the apex of a curling V and begin a wild ride up the side of one wave and down another. At the end of the rapid the boat is brimming with water. I turn and look upstream. The rapid graces the brown river with a beautiful white bodice of froth. Seconds later the river carries me around a bend, and Granite is out of sight. As I float in the calm stretch between Granite and Hermit Rapids I bail gallons of water out of the raft.

When a rapid is entirely visible from above and easy to run I don't scout from shore. Instead I look the rapid over from my raft, gaining about three feet in height by standing on the ammo boxes tied in front of my seat. It usually works, except for the time when I should have scouted but didn't, and ended up in the wrong place at the wrong time.

On the tenth day of a thirty-day trip, with Hance and lunch behind us, the group of twelve people and five boats floated into the Inner Gorge toward a cataract appropriately named Sockdolager. Like a lioness stalking her prey, the river flows downward into a glassy tongue until, in one swift, violent motion, it erupts into a curling reversed V—waves that tower fifteen to twenty feet—exploding and crashing down upon themselves. I was an overenthusiastic neophyte rowing *Sunshine Lady* for the first time in the canyon and I knew I should scout. But the others did not stop, and since I had no idea where to find a vantage point, I followed the leader.

We slid down the tongue in formation. The first raft disappeared in the apex of the V and was buried beneath crashing whitewater. "Oh shit!" I muttered, not bothering to watch what happened to the second raft. Frantically, I pulled on my oars. "Hang on," I shouted to my passenger Jeff as I pointed the raft's bow into the left side of the V. I threw my strength against the oars and felt the raft shudder as she met the wall of water and slid up the face of the wave. It was the right thing to do, the wrong place to do it. Hidden behind the back side of the wave was another wave, perpendicular to the first. I looked up and knew we were doomed.

Green, swirling water blotted out the day, tossing me around like clothes in a washing machine. I surfaced into dim light, the top of my head bumping against the thwart. I quickly ducked my head under the tubes and a moment later bobbed up next to the upside-down raft. Jeff's head surfaced near mine, his knuckles white from his death grip on the raft, his face twisted in fear. Wave after wave buried me, leaving me gasping for air, then coughing and choking. "Jeff, help me," I yelled, while I struggled vainly, again and again, to pull myself up the slippery tubes to the floor of the boat. "I can't," he screamed, "I'm tangled in the bow line." A chill, worse than the fifty-degree temperature of the river, ran through me. Then, without warning, the raft swung around and launched us toward a glistening black wall. I raised my feet in a futile attempt to keep from being crushed, when just as suddenly the boat twirled away from the rock. Prodded by fear, I grappled with the raft until I found a foothold on a submerged oar and heaved myself on top. I crawled to Jeff, still struggling to untangle himself, and with more strength than I thought possible, pulled him up on the bottom of the boat with me.

Relief brushed over me with a comforting hand as the first boat tossed us a line. Securing my raft to his, Stewart pulled hard into an eddy. "We're safe," I said, and Jeff smiled. Safe until the D-ring on Stewart's boat tore loose, releasing us to the current. Clinging to the underside of the boat, shivering uncontrollably in the first stages of hypothermia, we drifted into a small rapid. *What's next?* I wondered, but that was answered when the river calmed and Jeff tossed the line back to Stewart. A moment later we swirled around an eddy, five rafts and two kayaks, an adrenaline-charged flotilla.

With my boat hemmed in securely by the others, I abandoned it and jumped across the tubes toward a thermos of hot chocolate. While Jeff and I sat sipping the scalding liquid, Stewart leaped on my overturned raft and attached a flip line to the frame. "C'mon guys," he yelled, "let's get this over with." With a laugh and a shout, the others joined him. The boat rose out of the water, like the trap door of a storm cellar, as their weight pushed one side down while they pulled the opposite side up. The raft was perpendicular when Stewart announced, "You know this means we're all going to get wet!" A moment later five people disappeared in the river, and *Sunshine Lady* floated upright.

I glanced over my load. It was tied as firmly as it had been that morning, cleaner and wetter, but nothing lost—a consolation prize to soften the embarrassment of the flip. I looked away, then spread myself out on a slab of schist like a pagan sacrifice to the gods, soaking in solar radiation.

"Well, Patch, you've crossed the line."

"How's that, Stewart?"

"When it comes to flips, there's only two kinds of people: those who have and those who will."

Hermit Rapid, with its symmetrical waves and straight-forward chute, is one of the prettiest rapids in the canyon. Beginning with a wave about seven feet tall, each succeeding wave is taller, until the fifth one, which often reaches a height of twenty feet. Then in orderly fashion, the waves diminish in the same way they built up. They resemble ocean breakers in size and form, with one important difference: In the ocean the waves move while the water remains stationary; on a river the waves are stationary while the river moves.

Smoothly, effortlessly, I slide down the tongue, the bow of the raft descending at a sharp angle into the glossy trough. Magnetically the wave draws me to itself as illusion and reality blend and entwine. Briefly the raft stalls, then mounts the face, kissing the foam-tipped haystack before gliding down the back side. One wave follows another, a ride of rhythm and motion, dancing and swaying, rising and falling. The fifth wave holds itself erect like a soldier proud of her bearing. We mount the steep face and hang on top, suspended on the curling crest. A scream ascends above the roar of the rapid. A long, high-pitched wail, seemingly distant and apart from myself, but coming from some unknown place within me, simultaneously connecting me to and releasing me from the river, the canyon, myself.

The rapid is over. I bail the knee-deep water out of the raft.

I pass Boucher Rapid.

I bail.

In the distance, against a black wall darkened by its own shadow, a fine, almost imperceptible mist ascends out of the river. Far above the mist and the occasional splash of water leaping high into the air, far above the sound that resembles the roar of fans in a stadium, I pull *Sunshine Lady* over to the right shore. Involuntarily my stomach muscles tighten.

The rapid that causes the mist to hang heavy in the air is a legend. A Sagittarius with a reputation. Before December 7, 1966, she contained burbles and bubbles and not much more. Then a heavy storm moved over the North Rim and dropped fourteen inches of rain within a thirty-six-hour period, turning the side canyon into a raging monster. The flood wiped out pueblo sites that had existed for nine hundred years and washed a fan of boulders into the river, giving birth to a wild child known as Crystal Rapid.

Crystal's fame grew, and for more than sixteen years she terrified boaters with a nightmarish hole and a rock garden. The hole snuggled against the left wall just below the mouth of Slate Creek, randomly mushrooming twenty feet above its trough before crashing in upon itself like an explosion gone awry. The rock garden, downstream from the hole, loomed in the center of the river with naked fangs of granite and schist.

As if dissatisfied with her notoriety, in 1983 she expanded to awesome proportions. That summer the Colorado River peaked at ninety-two thousand cfs. Giant boulders rumbled beneath the raging waters, and a new hole, rising to heights of forty feet, formed a barrier across the gateway of the rapid. Within a week Crystal demolished seven thirty-three-foot pontoon motor rigs and killed one person. More than one hundred people had to be evacuated from the canyon by helicopter.

Boatmen and women prayed for the flood to transform Crystal. Their prayers were answered. When the high water subsided, the old hole was gone, replaced by a solid wall of water at her entrance that can lead straight to hell.

Once upon another time, on a trip before the 1983 transformation, I scouted Crystal with a group who had a lot of experience on other rivers but very little in the canyon. While the rest of the party discussed a jarring run through smaller holes to the right of Crystal Hole, I fixed my gaze on the Highway, an unruffled ribbon of current, perhaps eight to ten feet wide, slicing between the hole and the right run. The big guys' run, the run that required precise timing and nerves of steel. The run that combined the irresistible with the terrifying.

For a long time the group was silent, then Mark declared, "The only run is far right. Anything else is suicide."

"Yeah," Larry agreed, "I don't want to be anywhere near the hole."

"What about the Highway?" I asked. Eleven pairs of eyes examined me as if I'd just arrived from outer space.

"You want to go over there, we'll watch from shore," Mark said.

"Ha! Trash City. Let me get my camera," Larry snorted.

"Don't try it, Patch," Greg said. "I'm not going to do it."

I wondered what that had to do with me. I studied the Highway again.

"Where exactly are you planning to go?" my passenger Lisa asked. Our life jackets bumped up against each other.

I pointed out the route. "I'm sure I can do it. As long as we don't get into the haystacks above the hole we should be okay." I bit my lip. "I did it last year with no trouble."

"I believe you," she said, and cast her big brown eyes up at me. "But please don't miss."

"I'll do my best."

"I'm ready," I said to the rest of the group.

"You going for it?" Greg asked. I knew he was genuinely concerned.

I nodded.

"Want me to be the lead boat?" This would put him in a rescue position should I flip.

I nodded again.

The others looked at me in disbelief. "We'll stay here and

watch the show," Mark smirked.

I marched back to my boat, my stomach overrun with butterflies, my mouth laden with cotton fluff. I tied up the bow line and handed it to Lisa, then climbed over the gear to my seat. Sitting still, I closed my eyes, took a number of slow deep breaths and said a silent prayer to the spirit of the river.

Greg waved and rowed away from shore. When he was thirty or forty feet ahead of me, I pulled evenly on both oars, rowing *Sunshine Lady* to the middle of the river. Then, with a Double-Oar Pivot, I turned the boat one hundred eighty degrees, facing the boat's stern toward the right side of the tongue. I would row hard to gain momentum, break through two or three small holes, pivot the bow downstream and allow the Highway to carry me past Crystal Hole, giving her right edge a kiss as I went by.

It was a good plan and it went like clockwork. I was exactly where I was supposed to be. I powered through the small holes. I relaxed. I allowed the bow of the boat to turn slightly downstream toward a cauldron of exploding waves. Something was wrong. Things didn't look right. In less than a fraction of a second I recognized everything. I was too far left—

on top of the current that went directly into Crystal Hole.

Sheer panic churned my brain to mush. Sprouting wings seemed the only escape. Instinctively I pivoted the raft, turning the bow directly downstream, and lay every ounce of my one hundred fifteen pounds hard against the oars. *Sunshine Lady* responded, gliding up and over one haystack, then another, until we slid down the back of the final wave into the yawning curve of the Hole, which opened wide like a mythical monster and swallowed us whole.

Tons of water buried us in a liquid night, buried us with a force that shook *Sunshine Lady* to her thwarts and ripped the oars from my hands. I waited for the surge of water that would flip us, waited helplessly in the belly of the whale until slowly, very slowly, she regurgitated us to the topside of the hole. An eternity passed up there in the rarified air on the crest of a wave that surged beneath us. Then, with the power of a shot-put, she catapulted us downstream.

Lisa and I remained motionless for what seemed a lifetime. Then her scream pierced the air. *"We ran Crystal Hole!! We did it!! We did it!!"* She danced in waist-deep water, laughing and screaming.

I lunged for my oars, then sat on my rowing seat trembling

until a scream was wrenched from my throat and I joined her in announcing our feat to the world. "We did it, we did it, we ran Crystal Hole!"

After the worst of the waves subsided, Lisa and I hugged in ecstatic joy. Then I glanced upstream. No, Lady, we didn't run you. You were kind and forgave our absolute audacity. Still, I laughed. "Bail!" I yelled. "Bail."

Now I face other challenges: the stark emptiness of solitude and a vulnerability greater than the perils of flipping or dying. I'm more alone than I have ever been before. On previous trips I had someone else with whom to confer and share the excitement and apprehension. Which leaves me in a unique situation: I'm alone and I'm not going to wait for someone else to show up.

Fear erupts like the exploding waves in a rapid; rowing Crystal is suddenly unthinkable. My shoes are lead weights, affixed to this rock I'm standing on. Stuck once again. What difference does it make where it happens or what causes it? Fear is a prison door waiting to confine me when I give in to it. All my fears congregate, each one clamoring for attention. Fear of being confined and losing my freedom. Fear of loving, fear of being intimate and exposing myself to another. Fear of rejection. Fear of being dependent on another. Fear of leaving a job I hate because it provides security. Fears that cause me to create excuses for my contradictory behavior, to spend months searching for an ideal, then run from it as soon as it is within my grasp.

I've tried burying my fears in the sand and writing them on a piece of paper to be thrown into a fire. These symbolic acts struck me as a beautiful way to rid myself of my fears so I could be free. But my fears returned, stronger than they were before. All the running and burying and denying and excuses have not worked. Once again I'm plagued with fear and self-doubt as I stand above Crystal.

A sensible side of myself provides an excuse. A certain amount of fear can serve a purpose, honing me to a razor's edge so that I am keen and sharp and able to make fast, decisive moves. The secret is knowing whether I have crossed the thin line between having just enough apprehension to see danger clearly and being so overwhelmed by fear that I'm paralyzed. I think back to the first time I rowed Lava Falls. I was overcome with fear, until a friend told me to turn my negative energy positive by putting my fear into the river and not allowing it to disarm me of my power. My run through Lava that day was excellent.

"Your fear has very little to do with my ferocity," Crystal declares. "The hole is no larger than it was when you went through it years ago. It's your emotions you're afraid of, not me."

I nod. Her truth is too penetrating to ignore.

My emotional fears may not be as tangible as her rocks or holes, and they may be easier to deny, but by not dealing with them I'm running the same rapid over and over, going into the same holes that continually tear me apart. I'm repeating mistakes by not looking at myself and accepting the fears that are part of me. They need to be acknowledged in the same way that the river's obstacles require attention. Fears must be embraced, treated like friends instead of enemies, acknowledged in the same way I respond to whitewater—with reverence and respect.

I watch the river roll by, and as I study Crystal, my perspective changes. I've stopped coming apart. She is steadying me, bringing me back to reality and away from the illusory world of fear.

When I first met Mother River, I realized immediately that she was a source of knowledge for me. As a beginner, I'd sit in an eddy behind a boulder in the middle of a rapid, fascinated by the water's motion. I wanted to learn to row well, and as I learned, I gained a sense that if I managed my life the same way I guided a raft through a rapid, I would be very successful. When I rowed too hard and fought the current, I usually didn't get where I wanted to go. Or worse, I might be thrown out of the boat into the river, where I was truly helpless. If I let the boat go without guidance, I was no better off. As my rowing improved, I came to understand that using the river's strength, direction and flow helped me more than absolute control or total passivity.

I uproot my feet and walk along the edge of the river, studying the rapid, picking out a particular curl of a wave, a pillow of water as it flows up on a rock. I examine each subtlety until it is established firmly in my memory, and there is no chance I will get lost when I begin my run.

Back at *Sunshine Lady*, I tuck things away, untie and gently shove off. I float slowly downstream, holding the raft just outside the eddy that hugs the right shoreline. As I near the head of the rapid, I pivot the raft, turning the stern downstream at a forty-five-degree angle to the current, which gives me additional power when I pull on the oars. It is at this moment, on the edge of the rapid, that everything else disappears. I am totally focused—nothing else matters, nothing else exists. Everything blends together: Even *Sunshine Lady* no longer exists of her own entirety, but instead becomes part of me, and the two of us together become part of the rapid.

I hug the right shoreline, skirting smooth stones and small holes, neither pushing the river nor allowing her to sweep me away. I pass by Crystal Hole with more than a boat-length to spare, awed by her power and majesty. Maybe I have finally learned to acknowledge and accept my fears, learned that they are more like a collection of rapids than the monsters I make them out to be. If I can deal with them as I do rapids, I may even learn something about my own vulnerability.

At the bottom of the rapid I catch an eddy and look back upstream. This river is my mother and she loves me. I'm certain of that.

The Jewels glimmer and gleam, boil and roll between schist and granite walls rising straight out of the river. There's Agate, Sapphire, Turquoise, Ruby and Serpentine—boisterous, churning scamps who would be given more respect if they were situated at the beginning of the canyon instead of coming as they do after Crystal. Crystal diminishes them, unjustly so, though they might actually be easier to run after encountering that great lady.

When the Jewels and I part company, I row for Lower Bass Camp, named after William Bass, one of Grand Canyon's eccentrics, who operated a tourist camp in the early decades of this century. It is a spacious place to stay, lying at the base of an open arena where the Grand Canyon series of rocks is exposed for a short distance, along with a fault zone that tears open the impassable walls.

At the last possible moment, I catch the eddy and slide toward a grove of tamarisk trees that grow directly in front of the landing site. Behind the trees the camp opens up, first as small secluded areas surrounded by low walls of schist, then into a wide expanse with terraced spots overlooking the river. With more time and energy I'd hike the trail that leads up to a saddle, then down the other side to Shinumo

Creek, where a natural rock alcove houses relics from Bass's original camp.

Thousands of stars, acting as handmaidens to a full moon, entice me to eat a leisurely dinner and relax beneath the celestial magnificence. I untie and carry the usual paraphernalia to the beach, glance over the menu, then spread out my ground cloth, pad and sleeping bag and fall onto them like a rag doll.

Vague dreams of being cold plague me throughout the night, keeping me huddled in one position and causing my arms to become numb, then tingle with pins and needles when I move. In the morning, I wake less rested than the previous night.

After a huge breakfast I goad myself to take a walk, but like a horse that does not want to leave the stable, I plod slowly along. Wisdom dictates I stay at Lower Bass Camp an extra day and sleep away my exhaustion, but I decide to continue, and after my walk I take off, moving slowly and lazily downriver. A half-dozen moderately sized rapids with a few good waves provide a nice ride and demand little skill. When the river calms and meanders through quickly disappearing Schist and Granite, I ship my oars, letting the river carry me along.

I stop at Royal Arch Creek and follow a path that takes me around and over a jumble of house-sized boulders, next to a pool pregnant with algae and tadpoles, across a trickle of lukewarm water into the first of five levels of enchantment. Walls garlanded with maidenhair ferns and crimson monkey flowers reach up on three sides to touch the sky, and a slender stream of water falls more than fifty feet in tiers.

Shouts of glee echo off the walls as I recall other trips when people, young and old, swam under the waterfall into a cool grotto, then climbed up to a moss-padded ledge. Trembling with excitement and the chill that comes with water and shadows, they hesitate, then leap into the air, arms raised, hair streaming behind them, until they are swallowed by the night-green pool.

The shouts subside when I close my eyes and the ghosts of Elves Chasm swirl around me. The walls invite me to climb them to the next level, then the next, to immerse myself in splendor that flourishes with each new tier obtained, until an impassable wall of Travertine stops my progress. *Not this time,* I relate silently, and lean against a wall to absorb the magic that hangs heavy in the silence.

A moment later a couple of gossipmongers startle me out of my reverie. Chirping and bobbing, chirping and bobbing, two water ouzels discuss the events of the day. When I move slightly they look at me aghast, fly a short distance, bob a couple of times, then return to the side of the pool.

"Sorry girls, I have to pass by." I take a step toward them, then another, before they fly up to a cliff out of my reach. I continue down the slope on the other side of the pool and stop before it is out of sight. Turning slowly I watch the dippers return, then bob and chirp, bob and chirp. I feel like an intruder.

I rustle up a quick lunch and head out again. Cirrus clouds streak across the sky, bearing tidings of a storm two or three days hence. I hope they're wrong. A few miles downstream I stop at Blacktail Canyon. It's a must-see place, a place more haunted than Elves Chasm, a place with ghosts as old as time. They hide in the cracks and crannies of the Great Unconformity: a geologic misstep where Tapeats Sandstone sits directly atop Vishnu Schist. A couple of million years are missing in that line between the two formations. Poof! Gone. Just like that. No wonder the ghosts in here are restless. I walk along Blacktail's narrow, crooked wash, with knee-deep pools and pebbles that insinuate themselves into my shoes, until I'm stopped by a cul-de-sac. I'm tempted to sit on a rock and contemplate life: what's missing, what isn't, what great unconformity interrupts my own growth. I turn and walk back to my raft.

Immediately after Blacktail Canyon, large sandy camps that had been commonplace disappear beneath an inhospitable rock-strewn shoreline. I row 122 Mile Rapid and get soaked when one of the waves splashes over the side of the raft. Clouds close over a feeble sun, and I anxiously scan both banks for sign of a landing site. Places I remember camping in previous years are gone, buried under high water. In a careless move through another rapid, I get soaked again.

My fingernails turn blue, my skin is tight with goose flesh. I need a camp now. "Now," I shout. "Not in an hour or next week. Now."

Another mile passes under my raft, then two. Fossil Rapid is next. A squirrelly piece of whitewater. I search the shoreline frantically, looking for any hint of a place to pull over. Nothing! I float closer to the top of the rapid, then see a minuscule landing spot between rocks and tamarisk trees.

I stumble off the raft. With the little energy I have left, I devour a simple dinner, then crawl into my sleeping bag, leaving the dirty dishes lying on the sand.

I toss and turn, searching for sleep, which eludes me. Finally I give up and look at the moon. The moon looks back.

I'm losing it. One moment I'm as satisfied as a cat with a bowl of cream, the next I howl like a pup caught in a trap. I'm tired of being alone, tired of doing all the work day after day by myself, tired of not having anyone to talk to, maybe even tired of being in the canyon. I've obviously taken on more responsibility than I can handle. Look at the risk I took tonight, staying on the river too late. My imagination conjures up a hodgepodge of disasters. I'm no longer sure I can make it to Pearce Ferry. A tear slides down my cheek at the thought of failing at something that means so much to me.

I push off and run Fossil Rapid. Within a mile the walls close in, leaving me in the narrow, beachless canyon I dreaded entering last night. The river swirls and churns, compressed by the horizontal strata of the Tapeats Sandstone, which gives the illusion the river is racing downhill. I pick up speed and enter the middle Granite Gorge, gliding next to huge chunks of schist that glisten like polished onyx.

I run 128 Mile Rapid, staying out of the strong eddies at the bottom of the drop. On to Specter and Bedrock Rapids. After passing through the narrow channel to the right of the house-sized boulder that forms Bedrock Rapid, the canyon opens up again.

A mile and a half farther the roar of Dubendorff Rapid insists I stop and scout. I choose a route around rocks and holes and enjoy an exhilarating roller coaster ride over large waves. At the bottom of the rapid a large beach offers refuge.

A lone raven sails in upon my arrival, checking my credentials for landing, then flies away and does not return. An army of heavy, dark clouds marches swiftly across the sky on its way to wage war upon some hidden corner of the canyon.

Mice scurry under the table while I eat dinner, brazenly looking for food and examining my booted feet. When one crawls up inside my pant leg, I chase them away and go to bed.

Tonight no troubled thoughts, no uneasiness, drive away the sleep my body and brain demand. Tomorrow is a layover day. Life at this moment couldn't be better.

9

The Center

There is no such thing as a problem without a gift for you in its hands. We seek problems because we want their gifts.

— *Richard Bach,* Illusions: The Adventures of a Reluctant Messiah

This is the center and I've lost all sense of time. I don't know the day of the month nor the day of the week. I only know that Stone Creek marks the midpoint. Half my journey is behind me, half is still to come. Sometime back in antiquity I unrolled my boat, loaded my gear and said goodbye to Dee at Lees Ferry; somewhere in the future I'll reach Pearce Ferry, say hello to Dee and disassemble my raft. None of it has any relationship to me today. The past and future have ceased to exist.

It's easy to lose time in the canyon. Easy to lose other things too, like reality or myself.

Today I follow a trail beside Stone Creek, determined to go beyond my previous point of return. Immediately a waterfall cuts off my quest, forcing me to climb up the Bass Limestone—loaves of speckled rock stacked on top of one another—to join the creek once again. The creek rushes full and clean, providing me with a fresh drink of water along the way. Farther on, small trees droop, bushes cling to the ground and tangles of small logs and twigs embrace boulders and large cottonwood trees: evidence of a flash flood that occurred sometime this summer. Red mud is splattered everywhere in odd places, as though an artist went mad while painting this giant tableau.

Red, gray and dark fortresslike scarps tower above Stone Creek Canyon, creating a broad, expansive view. In a single moment the immensity of it hits me, and I shrink into insignificance; I am less than a particle of dust on a grand ballroom floor. Knowing that the area within my range of vision is only a small portion of the whole makes the total size of the canyon incomprehensible.

If logic ruled, this moment would be pervaded with

loneliness. But my loneliness has nothing to do with solitude. In solitude, especially the solitude of nature, I am complete. Rivers, lakes, trees, rocks and grand vistas of mountains or deserts, plains or sea, fill me with abundance. No, my
loneliness always grows from disconnection: feeling like an
outsider in a group I'd like to join, feeling undesirable or
unwanted by a man I desire, feeling out of place in a particular
environment, or feeling inadequate in some incomprehensible way that reminds me of my emotional vulnerability.

With sudden clarity, I realize that loneliness is the absence of love in one's life. Not idealized love, but loving one-
self. I'm lonely when I'm out of harmony with myself. I
look back over the days that have passed and the hints I've
received about the nature of my loneliness: choosing it because I'm frightened of love, not making commitments so I
can be free to follow someone else's lead, or living in a place
because it is considered ideal by others. One's habitat needs
to fit like a comfortable pair of shoes. Try hiking in boots
that pinch or rub, and your feet will be covered with blisters;
try living in a place that doesn't fit, and you'll sink into depression. Unfortunately, choosing the right place to live is a
lot harder than choosing the right boot. It's easy to become

enamored with a place's beauty or prominence. But making choices based on another's priorities robs you of your fundamental sense of self. I've been doing that, and I have neither the companionship I crave nor the freedom I seek. I go back and forth between isolation and gregariousness, briefly content with both, interminably dissatisfied with everything.

My canyon solitude has dissolved most of my loneliness. Loneliness hasn't stalked me; I haven't spent day after day longing for someone to be here with me. In the outside world, I drift through life feeling out of control, like I'm going into a rapid without oars. But here, with Mother River and Father Canyon, I am living the natural life I love. I am forced to meet my own needs. By coming here alone, I have refused to wait for someone else to do it for me. Each day I live with my own decisions, my own plan, even arguments with myself, without crumbling into nothingness. In the canyon I am powerful and autonomous, loving myself as I have never attempted to do before.

The simplicity is staggering. I never realized before that my loneliness is *mine*. It's so easy to expect other people to meet our needs and to not accept responsibility for dealing with our own loneliness. I've been looking to the outside world to cure the inside of me.

Willow trees sway in a light breeze. I take a leaf and slide my fingers down the length of it, noticing how it yields to my touch. When I let go of it, it hasn't changed; it is still a willow leaf, soft and yielding, yet strong and resilient— qualities I'd like to embody.

I continue to hike up Stone Creek Canyon and am rewarded at every bend. A wall of red shale, sparsely flecked with bright green plants, stands in sharp contrast to the subtle shades of beige and rose that predominate. When the creek shoots into the air before falling twenty feet into a churning pool, I am tempted, but only for a second, to plunge into this natural whirlpool and allow the falls to beat a powerful massage on my back. Here and there the water spreads out over shallow creek banks and slides sensually over moss-covered rocks. I fill my canteen near a large cottonwood tree, its golden leaves shimmering with reflected sunlight. At the base of a double waterfall I'm convinced my hike is finished, until I spot a cairn off to the right and follow the trail that leads up a cliff to the topside of the falls.

At the end of the climb the canyon narrows, and trees

and bushes choke the creek. I plow through, soaking my shoes and scratching my arms, drawn forward by the mystery of what lies around the next bend. A boulder blocks the way, and I struggle over it to enter a narrow passageway. With my fingertips touching both walls, I steady myself while my eyes adjust to the dim light. I have reached it, the end of the trail, stopped by the splendor of a stream of water sliding down a smooth, glistening rock wall covered with moss and algae.

I exit with the reverence I would accord a grand cathedral, sit on a rock in the sun and eat lunch.

The following morning I wake to a rich blue sky and red cliffs drenched in sunlight. I stare blankly, knowing it is time to rise, knowing without looking that *Sunshine Lady* is beached. The sound of the river is different, the noise level lower.

I remain in my sleeping bag, haunted by a dream.

I am at a roller skating rink with two men, one of whom I love. I sit on the sidelines while he learns to dance on skates. It's apparent that he is charmed by his teacher, a young, pretty woman. I feel left out but hope that when he finishes his lesson, he will return to where I'm sitting and give me the attention I crave. The other man is nearby. He is in love with me, but I ignore him in order to watch the man I love. After the first man finishes his lesson, he skates to a nearby bench and sits down, and the second man joins him. They sit with their backs to me, talking and laughing. Slowly I realize the man whose love and attention I want so badly does not care about me. The feeling of rejection is overwhelming. I wake as I unravel into nothingness.

Two men—one who loves me, one who doesn't. I scorn the first, ache for the second. It is so clear, so perfectly transparent. By falling in love with men who don't want me, I can always be free.

I am vulnerable and exposed, drained of all energy. The dream presents me with the pattern of my existence: waiting to be noticed by a man who doesn't care.

For a long while I lived on hope. Then when I happened to meet someone who was obviously crazy about me, I thought I had finally broken my habit of longing for disinterested men. I was excited and eager about our meeting, by the chemistry that electrified the air around us, by the compatibility of our preoccupations, by the merging of our words and bodies. I was excited until he began to pursue me at a feverish pace, suffocating me and cutting off my freedom. I found excuses to be alone; I found reasons not to persevere. I ended our brief affair as suddenly as it began, justifying my departure by enumerating his faults and ignoring my own.

The freedom I gained was soon replaced by a sense of failure. Everyone traveled in couples while I spent weekends alone in a popular bookstore, sipping cappuccino and reading books I didn't buy, before departing with the *New York Times* under my arm.

I was raised to get married and have children. That was the only life course I was allowed to consider when I was young. Yet I've never married and have only had a couple of relationships that lasted longer than a few months, and those were with domineering, controlling men.

Feeling uncomfortably hot in my sleeping bag, I slide the zipper partway down to let cool air in. It doesn't relieve the turmoil coursing through me. We women are quick to accuse men of being frightened of intimacy and commitment, but it's not a quality reserved exclusively for them.

Instead of making separate decisions regarding love, marriage, children, home and job, we lump them together as if
they are intrinsic parts of a whole. For many, they form the
perfect picture of contentment. But I associate this image
with being owned by someone, being controlled, being dependent. A snapshot that has kept me out of relationships
for fear of losing my freedom—or worse—losing myself.

There's nothing wrong with being independent or wanting to be free to travel and try new things. But I've carried it
too far. I guard my autonomy so closely I don't dare let a
man get near.

My fear of relationships runs so deep I can't remember
ever being without it. My mother spoke gloriously about
marriage and how wonderful it was to be pregnant. But from
early childhood I knew it was a lie. My father was off pursuing his hobbies and had no time for us, and my mother was
filled with rage, which she concealed beneath a phony de-
meanor. At an early age, she turned me into her confidante,
blaming me, my father, my developmentally disabled sister
and her mother for ruining her life. Though outwardly I
embraced the ideal of being swept off my feet by Prince
Charming, internally I learned that getting married and

having children was a fate worse than death.

I lie still for long silent moments, waiting for more insight. When nothing happens I rise, still shaken by the dream.

I eat a tasteless breakfast and ignore the river, the raft and the work that lies ahead. I hurt internally and cry outwardly.

Slowly I pack my bags, tent and kitchen, carry everything to the water's edge, then turn to *Sunshine Lady* and begin untying knots. Although there is a chill in the air, after a few moments I take off my clothes to relieve the oppressive heat. With gear on both sides of the raft I haul her toward the river, kicking and swearing when she will not budge.

When *Sunshine Lady* is floating, I reload the gear. I rant and rave and yell and fuss every time a line catches or the boat pulls away from shore. I scold the boat, the boxes, the rocks and the river with profanity and bad temper, as if they are deliberately trying to provoke me.

I continue my knock-down-drag-out fight with myself until, over the sound of my own shouts, I hear the drone of a motor. Looking up sharply, I meet the stunned eyes of two men gawking at me from a motor rig in the middle of the river. I look for a place to hide, knowing there isn't one, then glare back, wishing I could affix a curse on them for catching me exposed and vulnerable. When they don't move, I place my hand on my hip, smile and wave. Their awkward wave and the rev of their engine leave little to wonder about; when they glance back at my campsite, I know exactly what they are thinking:

"Did you see *that*?"

"Yep! Sure did!"

"Nutty as a fruitcake."

I'm tired and hungry and ready to settle down again, but instead I push off, not bothering to dress. A small plane flies downriver then banks steeply. "Haven't you ever seen a naked woman before?" I scream.

I only row when *Sunshine Lady* insists on going into an eddy, making me work hard to get back into the current. I shout at her again and again, telling her she is not being cooperative. One mile downstream I stop at Tapeats Creek to fill my water jugs with clear water. While on shore, I scout the rapid quickly, then carefully row up the eddy so I have room to pull into the middle of the river and thus avoid the holes and rocks on the side of the rapid. Once out in the current, I'm unable to find the spot I had located from shore.

I want to cry helplessly but instead maneuver the raft a little, stand up, look again and take a couple of quick strokes, narrowly missing a large hole that shoves the right oar off its thole pin. Hanging on to the oar with one hand, I guide the boat through the rest of the rapid with the other.

After a couple of small rapids the river calms and enters Granite Narrows. Schist and granite surface at the river again and for slightly more than a mile form the narrowest place in the canyon. Pretty pink and black. I ship my oars and sit back, allowing the boat to drift on its own.

My anger slowly subsides, leaving me off balance as if I've been attacked. No enemy but the one within, struggling to understand herself.

I reach over the side of the raft and swish a hand through the water. The river is as deep as my thoughts. The desire for love seems as essential as bread and water, finding and holding on to it as arduous as the trek up Mount Everest. And then some. We long to connect with someone then do everything we can to keep it from happening. Or if we do succumb to love, we treat it as if it were an enemy by erecting defenses, resisting the changes it brings about, finding excuses to keep ourselves separate. We seek perfection that doesn't exist until fear chases love into hiding.

I pick up the oars and row away from my thoughts. Hunger keeps me on edge. There's a camp on the right that provides a ringside seat to Deer Creek Falls. Quickening my stroke, I turn the boat and head for shore. The current grabs my raft and I slide steadily downstream but continue pulling hard toward the small, steep beach, miles and miles across a hundred feet of river. At the last possible moment, before slipping around a rock and away from the camp, I pull next to the bank. With the current still moving downstream, I grab the stern line and leap off the boat, falling against the sand on the steep beach. The line slips through my fingers as the boat moves away from shore. I recover, grasp the line, brace and reel in *Sunshine Lady*. When she is alongside the bank I tie her firmly to a tamarisk tree. I climb on board, rummage through boxes for food and a beer and eat ravenously.

The sun sets, turning the upper cliffs a fiery red. Beneath the top layers the lower cliffs darken, until near the river they lose dimension and become paper cutouts, silhouetted one against another. The western sky turns lavender before fading into darkness. Across the river, Deer Creek Falls changes in volume as I move about camp. Moon shadows dance with a cool but gentle breeze.

I leave the campfire and walk into the blackness of the night. The river gurgles like a baby in its crib, cooing about the pleasure it finds in being alive. To stand by the river, black in some places, shimmering silver light in others, affords me a peacefulness and love that are as close to perfection as anything in life can be. Perhaps this is all I really need.

A small brown spider crawls aimlessly back and forth, up and down, lost in the cream-colored walls of my tent. I follow her wanderings, decide she's not dangerous, then unzip the door of the tent and peek outside. The sky hangs in balance between night and day.

Absorbed by morning cleanup, I don't notice a dozen people glide by, silent as shadows, until out of the corner of my eye I see them land at the mouth of Deer Creek. They glance at me, then away, without acknowledgment. I feel slighted.

Fifteen people rummage through day bags, removing

cameras, binoculars, sweaters and hats in preparation for a hike to the top of Deer Creek Falls. Armed against any happenstance, they trickle off the rafts and make their way over the sand and through the stream to the start of the trail. Moments after their departure, a kayaker pulls in, slides out of the boat and begins peeling off layers of insulation. I watch as if I'm viewing a play. The person pulls the kayak on shore, discards the life jacket, removes the helmet and peels off the wetsuit, all the time facing away from me so I have no clue as to the person's gender. I expect the mystery to unravel with the clothing, but the slim figure with short brown hair, clad in shorts and a fleece top is androgenous. S/he moves around and I study each gesture until the subtle language of body movement reveals the feminine. Perhaps women and men are more alike than we wish to admit.

I throw the end of the bow line in the raft and row across the river. The woman greets me with surprise. I want to chat but even the simplest sentences prove as difficult as trying to speak a foreign language. I manage a few words and start up the trail, wondering if this trip has doomed me to be a hermit the rest of my life.

I climb up switchbacks on a steep talus slope, then follow

the path into a narrow canyon. A Tapeats Sandstone cliff rises sharply on my left, sometimes forcing the path to the edge of a forty-foot drop where the roar of rushing water ascends out of the darkness. When the trail tilts steeply toward the precipice, I hold my breath, as if that will make a difference, while I take cautious steps across. A little farther on, the canyon widens, and the trail converges with Deer Creek.

I've spent countless hours at upper Deer Creek, enjoying its natural sandstone benches, its small waterfalls and its pools, which provide a haven from summer's heat and blazing sun. When I've been here with others, we've climbed down the sandstone walls to the creek and wandered knee- and sometimes belly-deep in the stream. Our voices raised in laughter and song reverberated against the narrow walls; cool, moist air raised goose flesh on our arms and legs. Where the creek plunged over a twenty-foot falls, we turned back. Before climbing out of the canyon, we lingered on a stone bench in the sun at the base of a redbud tree. In another setting this tree would complete an exquisite garden display. Here wildness lends it an aura of strength and perseverance, for how else does something so delicate manage to thrive against the torrent of water that washes through here periodically?

The flash floods that come out of the expanse of desert above Deer Creek can instantly change the canyon. Serenity turns brutal. Trees are uprooted and huge slabs of sandstone crash into heaps of rubble, creating instability in upper Deer Creek Canyon. It's smart to be cautious here, to watch where you sit, and hope that you'll be like the man who rose from a nap minutes before his bed was buried under a two-ton rock, and not like the man who was killed when a stone fell from above and went through his chest like a bullet.

It's too cool to swim in the crystal clear pools, so after a short stay I return to the river along the same path, pausing at a landing that provides long views both up and down the river corridor. The other group has been swallowed up by time and space, leaving *Sunshine Lady* to occupy the beach alone.

I'm warmed by the hike, but as I run the riffle next to the mouth of Deer Creek Falls, a penetrating chill sweeps through me. I remove my life jacket and pull a sweater out of my day bag. Looking over deserted camps, I remember moments from other trips. I take no notice of what's ahead. I know this river, know where I am. The sweater catches on a barrette at the top of my head, and with my hands entangled in the sleeves and the wool over my eyes, I hear the deep-throated clamor of Doris Rapid. Now what sort of a lady would spring herself on me so suddenly? I grapple with the sweater, yanking it over my head, and throw my life jacket on. At the last minute I move *Sunshine Lady* into position. Large waves come at me from all directions. Within seconds I'm drenched and shivering.

I bail the water out of my boat, wondering how I'm going to get warm. Moments later I hear the whine of a motor rig.

He catches me quickly and shuts off his motor as he draws near. One boatman and nine male passengers, most with fishing rods, greet me in unison. "Hi!"

"Hello," I respond with a big smile. "What are you up to?"

"A fishing charter," the boatman answers. "Where's the rest of your party?"

"This is it."

"Want some company?" one man shouts.

"Yeah, I'll go with you," another offers.

"No, take me," a third counters.

I laugh. "It's okay, I'm enjoying the trip by myself."

"You're a brave one," a fisherman says. The others nod. I

glow like a schoolgirl under their praise.

"You look pretty cold," the boatman says. "Want a swig of brandy?"

"Thanks, that would be nice."

He leans out and down from his boat, which is considerably higher than mine, grabs *Sunshine Lady*'s frame with one hand and extends a small bottle of brandy with the other. His position is precarious, and I lean toward him to keep him from going overboard. As my hand grasps the bottle, I look into the bluest eyes I have ever seen. Surrounded by long, blond lashes, they sparkle with life. I hesitate, then gulp the brandy, once, twice, igniting a fire inside me. I take a third swig and hand the bottle back. As I do, the boatman releases my boat and the two craft drift apart. My head whirls from the brandy, the compliments and the nearness of those blue eyes.

When they leave, the cold returns. Rock-tumbled shores stretch up to high, straight walls that hem in the cold river and prevent the sun from reaching the interior of the canyon. I continue on to Kanab Creek where I find a beach just large enough for my tent.

I begin collecting dinner articles, then decide that a cup

of tea will be enough. I boil a pot of water on my little stove, brew the tea and crawl into the tent with a book. The same spider travels around the vast desert landscape of my tent ceiling, still wandering aimlessly and appearing confused.

The cold penetrates like a sharp knife, finding its way inside my clothes. I draw my sleeping bag around me. I'd like to believe it is this particular section of the Canyon, with its high, dark walls, that is making me so cold, but I know the chilly days are here to stay.

With the inactivity, my thoughts wander back to the morning at Stone Creek when my perceptions about relationships shook me to the core. Choosing solitude is normal for me. I've been traveling alone for years: trips to foreign countries, road trips in the United States, day hikes in the wilderness and shorter, less remote, river trips. The canyon trip is a natural extension of that, though it is more remote and dangerous than anything else I've ever done.

I enjoy solitude, sometimes more than I enjoy companionship, which makes me a bit of an anomaly. I grew up during a time when society proclaimed the world to be a dangerous place for women. Those of us who ventured out on our own were considered odd. The stigma of being alone is certainly greater for women born before the women's movement of the early seventies, and greater still for the pre-baby-boomer generations. Meeting young women in the nineties, who view marriage and motherhood as optional rather than requisite, who travel independently, or do any number of other things because it pleases them, is wonderful. Meeting older women who have broken away from the restrictions of their youth makes my heart soar.

Men, for the most part, have not been labeled peculiar when they go adventuring alone. Rather, they are considered brave and daring. Of course, by keeping women tied to the kitchen and bedroom, a man has someone to come home to, someone to swoon over his heroic deeds.

I'm not sure I blame them. I wouldn't mind having someone to return to, someone who would have my dinner waiting, give me a massage and listen to my exploits. Dee will be there for me at the end of this trip, but he's a friend, not a lover. I don't know of any women who have a boyfriend or husband keeping the home fires burning while they are out conquering the world, or even their own demons.

It's up to women, of course, to reverse it. If more of us proclaim our independence, men will change, as many men in their twenties have already done. Some of them might even prefer tending the home fires rather than seeking to be Mr. Macho.

After years of going it alone, I'm not sure I'm capable of cohabitating with someone. There are some of us who simply can't be tied down. It's a positive response to our nature rather than a negative reaction to our past. To suppose that coupling is the only healthy, normal thing to do is harmful and untrue. My restlessness and need for change, my curiosity to see the world, may make me an unsuitable mate.

The next morning I start up Kanab Canyon, hoping to revive my flagging energy with an invigorating hike. Within minutes the path enters a pool. I remove shoes, socks and pants and wade in. The water tickles my belly button. I dress but moments later remove my shoes and socks again and roll up my pant legs to wade through yet another pool. I want a hike, not a swim, but time after time the path is cut off by a sheer wall, forcing me to cross the creek. My preoccupation with keeping my shoes dry soon zaps what little energy I have. A mile up Kanab Canyon I stop at a spring trickling from the top of a travertine cliff. An opulent cloak of soft moss, green ferns and crimson monkey flowers spills off the side of the wall. I finger the leaves and flowers and moss, fill my water bottle, then head back to camp.

Soon after I arrive the sun peeks from behind the South Rim, illuminating my home like a spotlight on a stage.

A moment later, a boat glides by on the other side of the river, a large blue raft carrying four bundled-up souls. As the raft rocks through Kanab Rapid a yellow boat appears, then an orange one, then another and another, each skimming by on the fast current. No one notices me, for both my boat and camp are hidden behind tamarisks and large rocks. I stop cooking and watch each raft as it passes, wondering where they are headed at this late hour. With the sixth boat the fleet ends, leaving no trace other than the subtle change within me. The canyon is no longer mine alone.

10

Retrospection

Events are absorbed and become a part of who we are. To attempt to get over them is as futile as to keep living them.

— *Marybeth Holleman, "The Wind on My Face" in* Solo: On Her Own Adventure

I glide through the riffle next to Olo Canyon and wave at the group of many-colored boats camped in the alcove. Automatically, I look to the rear of the camp where a stream of water drops twenty-five feet off the lip of an overhang into a small pool. The rope is still there. My stomach lurches, my mind fills with memories. Olo still haunts me.

The upper reaches of Olo Canyon would be inaccessible to all except the most experienced climbers if it weren't for that rope. It slithers off the lip of the overhang, luring people

to it as if it were charmed, and makes the climb look decep-
tively easy. If you're brave enough—or foolish enough—to
climb up the regularly spaced loops and over the lip, you
enter a tight grotto with a deep pool. At first glance it looks
like a cul-de-sac, but near the edge of the overhang you can
find toe- and handholds and ascend fifteen feet up this wall
to enter a large, beautiful amphitheater with smooth sculpted
stone, small pools and a moss-padded waterfall. It's impossible to stop here, and so you continue up the waterfall to
still another level and another beyond. I've been up those
levels once, just once, and only because I had good friends to
help me. Many years after the accident.

On the twentieth day of a thirty-two-day trip, with the wind
doing everything it could to blow us back upstream, our
group stopped to make an early camp at Olo. Ten tired people
with short tempers unloaded boats and set up camp.

I found a niche next to a boulder and spread out my
ground cloth and pad, then sat down and buried my face in
a book, happy to be away from a group that grated on each
other like sand in a sneaker. The sort of trip that made me

wish for solitude. Moments later, voices bouncing off the back wall caught my attention.

Six of the crew stood at the base of the rope. Their voices rose and fell with enthusiasm and concern as they discussed climbing to the next level. How could they even consider such a difficult climb, I wondered. They had to be dead tired.

"It's not that hard," Mike said, his voice scraping the air.

He snatched the rope and fitted his foot into the first loop, hauling himself upward. The rope stretched, then swung under the lip, tilting his back to the ground. Undaunted, he climbed up the sisal and over the lip. He disappeared for a few seconds, then bent over and waved to Greg. Greg put his foot into the first loop, tested the swing of the rope, then went up another loop and stopped. Looking up at Mike, he shook his head and retreated.

Diane stepped up next, eagerness pouring out of every cell in her body. She fingered the sisal, listened to Greg and asked questions I could not hear. His head wagged, his hand cautioned her. She appraised him, then looked up at Mike, who waved her on. I wasn't surprised when she grabbed the rope, but I was dismayed. I didn't think she had the strength or ability to execute the climb. Slowly, loop by loop, she struggled to the lip. There she hesitated, one foot in a loop, the other dangling, one hand clinging to the rope, the other groping over the lip for a handhold. Her back muscles bulged as she strained to maintain a grip. Mike, his red hair and beard standing out against the beige limestone, extended his hand. Her fingers grazed his. I turned away, unwilling to watch the inevitable.

It was a hard, flat sound. The splat of a firm, yet soft, body landing on a very hard surface. Only the silence screamed.

It took a second or two, no more, before Greg jumped into the pool where she had slid, braced Diane's head and shoulders and turned her over. She stared with unseeing eyes into the blankness of the gray sky. Thin lines of blood trickled from her mouth, nose and ear. An unearthly moan—a wail of deep, internal pain—escaped her throat.

I dashed to the scene and each of us, intent on doing the utmost to help, mentally flipped through the pages of the first-aid book.

"Don't move her. Don't move her."

"Oh God! Oh God!"

"Get the first-aid kit."

"Keep her still."

"Get the deck off the back of my boat."

"Gently now."

"Don't move her."

"Hold her legs steady."

"All together now—steady, steady."

"Take it easy, I'm slipping."

"Where should we go?"

"Under the ledge, under the ledge where it's level."

"Can we carry her that far?"

"Easy! Easy! I said easy, dammit!"

"Try not to jar her."

"I'm trying, dammit!"

"Get a tarp and set it up to protect her from this damn wind. C'mon, it's blowing sand all over the place."

A year's length of seconds later we set Diane, bleeding, moaning and unconscious on the sand. Unspoken questions darted between eyes round and tormented with worry.

"Her neck could be broken and she probably has a fractured skull," Larry, fresh from EMT training, whispered.

"Do you think she can hold out until we can get help?" someone asked.

"She has to, there's no other choice."

"This part of the canyon doesn't get air traffic," I reminded them.

Greg nodded. "Havasu is the only place we can get help."

"That's ten miles of rowing, and more than ten miles of hiking to reach the village. Is it possible to reach it tonight?"

"Greg and Mike are the best hikers. They should go."

While Larry looked after Diane, the rest of us raced to the beach, helped them tie down gear and shoved them out against the eddy waves. Greg dipped the oars and pulled hard, pulled again, then stopped when the whine of an engine announced the arrival of a motor rig.

"We've had an accident, a bad one. Do you have a radio or a doctor aboard?" Greg screamed.

"No, we don't," a bearded, blond man, his hand on the tiller, answered. "What happened?"

"A woman fell from the top of the rope. She looks pretty bad. We think she might have a broken neck and a concussion. Can you take us to Havasu?"

"We were planning to stop before then," he answered.

"We'll take you down," another man interjected. "Hop on."

Greg and Mike jumped on the motor rig and they zoomed

out of sight.

"They're both good hikers. They just might be able to get to Havasu village before dark," someone said, without a trace of hope in his voice.

"Yes," the rest of us murmured.

Tending the sick is not my strong suit. Pain and blood turn my mind to mush, my speech to gibberish, my hands inept. I stood aside and watched the others soothe Diane when she gained consciousness. I saw death; they told her everything would be okay. When she asked me, the only other lens wearer in the group, to remove her contacts, I jumped at the chance to be useful. Once the lenses were out and safely put away, I faded into the background, following the instructions of those more adept than I.

Darkness settled over the camp. Furtive shadows dodged around the sickroom as flashlight beams stalked the night. We stood nearby, uncertain if Diane's moans and thrashing were a blessing or a curse. Larry prodded her and questioned her, trying to determine the extent of her injuries.

"I don't think her back or neck are broken," he said.

"She's moving around too much for that," someone else agreed.

"It hurts when she breathes; she could have a punctured lung." Larry's face was taut. "We need to raise the backboard, make her breathing easier."

We returned to her side.

"Put a pad under me," she pleaded in ragged tones.

Larry nodded and we slid it under her before placing the top of the board on a box. Her moans and thrashing decreased.

We watched over her in two-hour shifts throughout the night. "You look awful," she said to me once. I'm sure I did. I thought she was going to die. By early morning Diane began to slip into sleep, and the wind and rain let up.

We searched the sky for the helicopter we hoped would find us. Thick, dark clouds crowded over the narrow space of sky visible between the canyon walls.

"What if they didn't make it to the village last night?" a voice of doubt asked at breakfast.

"How long does it take to do the hike?"

"Even running most of the way, I don't think it can be done in less than two and a half hours."

We waited, our heads tilted back searching the sky, our ears perked for the first sound of the whirlybird's rotor.

It appeared without warning, flying high over our camp,

and quickly disappeared. We screamed and waved and nearly collapsed in grief. They hadn't seen us; they'd never find this tiny spot in this vast canyon. Then we heard it, the wump, wump, wump, nearly deafening, as the helicopter hovered, huge and powerful, over our heads. We dashed for cover behind boulders while the copter blasted sand everywhere. When it settled, two men in orange coveralls, carrying a large case and a stretcher, vaulted out of the bird. A pilot with ice blue eyes, looking more like he was on a mission in Vietnam than on a rescue trip in the canyon, remained in his seat.

"Sorry for the delay," one of the men said. "We've been trying to take off since five-thirty this morning but the storm wouldn't let us. As soon as it broke we went up." The man speaking motioned toward the pilot. "This guy can fly that bird through the eye of a needle, but flying through a storm in the canyon is suicide."

They scurried to Diane, our group hot on their heels.

"How are you doing?" the head paramedic asked.

"Not bad," Diane answered. "I'd sure like a drink of water. These ogres haven't let me have a drop all night."

"Good for them," the man answered. "Sounds like they know what they're doing."

"Oh great! Just what I need, more sadists."

The paramedic smiled. "We'll give you something better." He inserted an IV.

"I'm going to have to cut your bathing suit off," the other man said.

"Just my luck," Diane countered. "Two handsome men, and I'm in no shape for sex."

They poked and prodded her before covering her with a sleeping bag.

"We have to move her to the stretcher," one man said. "We'll need your help."

We lined up on either side of her and slid our hands carefully under her back, neck, head and legs.

"On the count of three, everyone lift together."

"One . . . Two . . . Three . . . Lift!"

Diane's scream ricocheted off the walls.

"I'm sorry sweetheart, but we had to do it. It'll be smooth from here on out."

The two paramedics picked up the stretcher and carried her to the helicopter. We hovered like worried parents as they flattened a seat and laid the stretcher across it.

"You did everything right. You saved her life," one of the

men said before squeezing back into the whirlybird.

We watched it lift off, waited in the rain until it disappeared, then packed up and made our way downriver, stopping five miles short of Havasu.

"Greg and Mike are probably waiting for us," I said.

"We're tired, we've had a long night," the trip leader answered.

"So have they," I replied.

"They'd be stupid to be waiting at the river."

"We told them we'd pick them up," I said.

"Well, this is as far as we're going."

That night it poured. The following afternoon we arrived at Havasu to find Greg and Mike waiting on the rocks, having spent a cold, wet night without warm clothes or shelter.

I drift with the current, my eyes never leaving Olo, remembering that day clearly, remembering how we spoke about the accident in different voices and with varying opinions for the rest of the trip, remembering how it affected our dreams and our feelings for one another. And the questions, the questions that arose then and arise still today.

I am troubled less by Diane's fall than I am by what happened before and after her accident. Although the group had never been cohesive, other than the one night we worked together to save Diane, her accident split us sharply. Three people believed the group was an entity and therefore everyone was accountable to the others. Six declared they would do as they wished regardless of how the others felt. Where is the line that allows a person to explore his or her potential and enjoy freedom of expression without becoming inconsiderate and a burden to other people? By choosing to travel with a group, do we also choose to abide by the group's rules at the expense of our own freedom?

I ponder these questions as my boat glides along on a swift river. Both sides—complete freedom or group loyalty—have merit if we're willing to accept responsibility for our actions. If we take risks and fail, are we willing to bear the price, even if it means death or serious injury? If we want to travel with a group, are we willing to give up a certain amount of freedom for the safety and companionship it provides? If we go against the group's wishes and encounter difficulty, do we expect others to pick up after us? However we behave, whatever we choose to do, are we willing to accept the consequences?

When I asked for permission to solo the canyon, the

District Ranger said, "People should have that option." I agree with him. If I stumble over a rock and break my ankle, if I fall out of my raft in a rapid, if any number of things that *can* go wrong *do* go wrong, I could be in a serious predicament. I might even die. I hope I make it through without a scratch, but even if I don't, the decision to take this trip was mine to make. For me, the privilege of doing a solo trip through Grand Canyon greatly outweighs the risk.

As for Diane, she recovered from a fractured skull, eight broken ribs on her left side and a punctured lung. Death had spared her; its specter changed all of us.

A patch of sunlight streaks out of Matkatamiba canyon, laying a band of gold across the river. I'd like to suspend my forward motion in that ray of light, soak up the warmth it offers, but the current carries me through in a flash. The difference in temperature is remarkable. I look at the map. When the canyon turns north or south I can look forward to bands of sunlight filtering down to the river. When it travels west, deep shadow prevails.

A mile after Matkatamiba I hear Upset Rapid. I tie

Sunshine Lady to a needle-sharp piece of fallen Muav Limestone, all the time looking upstream, expecting to see the fleet of colorful boats come around the corner. When they don't appear, I walk downstream, over rocks, under ledges, past sacred datura plants and hidden mice homes, and look over the turbulence.

Where could they be?

The rapid presents one major obstacle—Upset Hole near the bottom of the whitewater—and two ways to miss it. Rowing cautiously along the right shoreline, I can bypass the hole easily, unless I pop an oar, miss some strokes or get hung up on a rock. Running the left side of the rapid entails dealing with large waves that roll off a sheer cliff.

I fidget.

Where are they?

I look back at the rapid. The left run always looks wilder from the right shore than it really is. But I've been there and know it's more fun and easier in some ways than the right run.

I look at the rapid; I glance upstream. Not a colorful raft in sight.

I stall. I'm nervous and waiting around doesn't help.

I amble back to my boat. Carefully, methodically, I check a line or two, put on my life jacket, coil the stern line. I stare upstream wishing a blue boat around the bend. Nothing.

I wonder what the hell happened to my confidence.

I pull to the center of the river, ship the oars and stand on the ammo boxes. I study the rapid. I float closer. Which way to go? Left? Right? Closer. Can't decide. Playing chicken with a rapid isn't the smartest thing I've ever done. I fold my arms across my chest while shimmering water draws me closer. Right? Left? I drop onto my rowing seat and push like hell to the left. The first reflex wave lifts the front of the boat and I slide over it. Another wave, then another, until I near the crazy turbulence next to Upset Hole. Large waves rear up, hit me sideways and for one interminable moment, bury me beneath their froth. When I surface I am beyond it all. The tail waves are fun, roller coaster fun. I laugh. I pass through another sun zone and remove a layer of wool. I bail, take photos and float.

Seven miles of tight canyon walls and calm river until lunch at the mouth of Havasu. I row from the Colorado's murky green water into the turquoise blue of Havasu Creek, between walls that curve outward, then in, like hands cupped together.

The Havasupai—people of the blue-green waters—occupy an idyllic section of Havasu Canyon about ten miles from the river. A trail runs alongside the creek, passing one cascade after another as translucent water flows over travertine ledges into deep pools. The abundance of water creates a lush, green paradise of cacti and grapevines, cottonwood and mesquite trees. Mooney Falls, two hundred fifty feet of falling white splendor, marks the final leg of the hike. To reach the village you must climb a massive flow of travertine that looks as if it belongs in a fantasy world and not on Mother Earth—the hike Greg and Mike did at a run to save Diane's life.

I eat lunch slowly, awaiting the other boats like an eager hostess. Finally, I put things away and untie the raft. As I row from the eddy into the current there's no sight of anyone else.

The nine miles from Havasu to National Canyon, my night's camp, go quickly in spite of the fact that I barely row other than to keep the boat in the current. After dinner I build up the campfire. It's a grand, old-fashioned fire, with bright orange and yellow flames licking the logs and reaching upward to the sky. It's too large and I know it, but the warmth and company it provides dispel any qualms I might have. This is a storyteller's campfire, a fire to tell jokes by, to share an intimate conversation with a friend, strum a guitar or listen to a plaintive song. A fire to sit alone and dream by, to enjoy as well with myself as with others.

National Canyon's dry, rocky stream bed covered with small, smooth stones narrows within a quarter of a mile. Clear water dribbles over and under large boulders that have fallen from the cliffs above. In places, the stream pushes its way through a narrow opening, then falls a few feet into a crystalline pool. Everywhere the continual flow of water over rock has carved and shaped the stone into highly polished sculptures. Exploring this side canyon resembles a stroll through an art gallery more than a hike in the wilderness.

I continue at a leisurely pace, climbing up a ledge or over a boulder now and again. Why hurry when I've come here to enjoy the absence of time? A cul-de-sac, created by walls that form a narrow chasm, soon cuts off my progress. From here on, it's vertical. I contemplate a tricky climb and choose to remain on the substantial, horizontal earth.

One quick snack and two miles farther downstream, I stop at Fern Glen Canyon. A long, gently sloping beach stretches from the river one hundred feet back to the canyon walls. Tamarisk trees clump together in small groups across the beach.

Two huge stone pillars, one on each side of the wash, guard the mouth of Fern Glen Canyon. Like two worn-out gate posts from a mythical giant's castle, they lean against the walls from which they originally fell. I walk past them into the canyon they guard, up a rocky wash, then follow a sharp bend to the left and enter a narrow, steep-walled passage.

Boulders clog the route, but I slither through their crevices like a lizard, to an alcove surrounded by walls with a ceiling of sky. Each wall in this thirty-by-fifty-foot cirque is distinctive from the others in texture and color. One is moist and calcified, dripping spring water through verdant ferns. Another, formed by gray, crumbly rock, is rough, while a third wall has a polished sheen like a soldier's boot. The fourth contains a house-sized slab of Muav Limestone perched at a precarious angle atop a boulder the size of a Volkswagen bug.

I walk over small, smooth stones no larger than my fist into the ambiance of a stately courtyard.

I hesitate before starting to the next level, knowing that coming down along the narrow ledges will be considerably more difficult than going up. Curiosity wins out, and I make my way upward to an even larger courtyard. Pink-beige walls, fern-draped ledges and a black-stained waterslide covered with moss and algae eliminate any possibility of continuing further. I cross a rock-strewn patio to lie on a smooth ledge and listen to the silence.

Surrounded by the tranquility of flowing water and secluded alcoves, I gaze up at the sky from the bottom of a bowl and drift into sleep.

When I wake, the remnants of a dream shake me to the core.

I am walking in a city with my best friend Sarah. She asks how my mother is. I reply, "My mother is like a cup of strychnine with cream on top. When you first taste it, it's sweet; then it kills you." Sarah nods, and we go on talking about mundane things.

I feel the stone terrace hard against my back. I search the walls, the sky, anything to break the horrific impact of the dream. How can any part of me portray my mother like that? Then, a sensation that begins deep inside me rises and spreads everywhere, until I know with every cell in my body how completely accurate my dream is.

I don't like to think about my mother. I have been beguiled by her charm, manipulated and lied to, disparaged and discounted more times than I care to enumerate. The immediate flash of anger that occurs when she first enters my thoughts is quickly replaced by pain, a pain that gapes like a fathomless black hole.

I remained for years under her dominion, siding with her against my father, doing the things she wanted me to do, dressing the way she wanted me to dress, being the person I thought she wanted me to be. Killing myself while waiting and hoping for her unattainable love and approval, all the time believing she had my best interest at heart, when nothing was further from the truth.

I sit up and bury my face in my knees. If your mother doesn't love you, then it's difficult to believe anyone can love you. That premise follows you into adulthood, influencing your choices from jobs to lovers. When families wrap so-called love in lies, mixed messages and rigid controls, genuine caring is an alien concept.

Love still frightens me and dreams present me with agonizing truths, but little by little this river and canyon have allowed me to claim my life as my own, to begin moving past my father's indifference and my mother's jealousy and hate. Understanding my relationship to it all is the only path to true freedom.

I approach *Sunshine Lady* swaying up and down rhythmically with the surges of river as it moves into shore. How tiny she is against the canyon walls and fast flowing river.

I am coiling the stern line, enjoying the essence of the canyon when I hear voices. I wait, line in hand, expecting to see the long-awaited boats. No one appears. With a shrug of my shoulders, I tie the line and toss it in the raft. Then once again I hear someone speak. I look around for the source, a creepy sensation crawling up my spine, but all I see is an open beach, a vacant river. I'm about to push off when the voices speak again. I stand motionless, listening with a sixth sense until the river, murmuring in quiet tones to herself, or me, or the countless animals and spirits that abide in the canyon, speaks again.

I need to move on but I don't want to break the spell.

She might not talk anywhere else. The voices continue, sounding like the soft murmur of a distant crowd. As I listen, I am drawn closer and closer, until I connect with the river and become part of her spirit, knowing something far beyond the ordinary world.

11

Canyon Spirits

Better a little danger than desperation.

— *Anonymous Boatman*

Lava Falls is the sort of rapid I run in my dreams months before the put-in at Lees Ferry and months after the thirty or forty seconds it takes to float down the slick, glassy tongue into a chaos that is burned into my memory. Situated alone on the river after miles of flat water and lazy riffles, Lava is the black-maned lion on the Serengeti plain, a humpback whale in the Pacific Ocean. It is neither subtle nor deceitful; it is truth in its purest form. It does not attempt to be something it is not, nor does it pretend to be greater than it is. Lava simply lives up to its reputation as the largest navigable rapid in North America.

I pack my raft with shaking hands as I listen to the river voices badger me with words of caution and hints of catastrophe. "You're all alone and Lava is just five miles downstream, less than two hours away, a few hundred strokes, that's all, a very short distance. Think you're ready to run Lava alone, Patch, ready for the ultimate solo experience?" I scowl. It would be an accomplishment; it's also dangerous as hell.

I continually look up, though I'm certain that no one else is near. The party of many-colored boats probably passed me yesterday while I was hiking up one of the side canyons. Still, I'm unable to relinquish my desire to crawl into the bosom of a group and nurse off the security of their presence. "Your run will be the same alone as it would be with others," Ma River declares. "Perhaps better. If you flip, you'll be forced to swim whether or not you have an audience."

"Thanks, I needed that," I retort.

Then swiftly, noiselessly, as if reading my thoughts, a big blue boat appears from around a bend in the river. The oarsman looks at me in surprise, then waves and shouts, "Hello!" As the current sweeps him away, he screams over the sound of the river: "Come have lunch with us." I nod my head vigorously.

In less than a minute, two more boats come around the bend. I tie up my stern line and push off to join them. Three boats follow behind me.

We move quickly downriver for a mile, remaining in formation, until the lead boat pulls over to a beach. The guides pull out a table and set up a stove to provide food and hot drinks for cold passengers.

I remain in *Sunshine Lady* grinning like the Cheshire cat as I move from total solitude into the middle of activity—no less alarming than zipping along an interstate during rush hour after driving on country roads for a month. After a lot of hesitation I walk to the periphery of the group and nod as people introduce themselves.

We talk in the high tones of people new to each other, eager to tell their stories, to impress, to entertain. "We put in on the Green River below Flaming Gorge Dam in Wyoming over fifty days ago and will take out at Pearce Ferry less than a week from now," someone tells me. "Incredible trip," another adds, "absolutely incredible." A third says, "We're duplicating Powell's original journey as near as possible. Quite an undertaking." I nod, maybe someday . . .

After a lunch of hot soup and sandwiches we're back on the river.

Vulcan's Anvil is the first hint of the terrific lava flow that plugged the river a million years ago. Like a lighthouse sentinel it towers thirty feet out of the river a mile above Lava Falls. We encircle it, placing a hand on the polished rock and patting it as if to gather strength from its massiveness. I open a box and take out a penny I've saved for this special moment and offer it to the river spirit. The bright copper piece glimmers in the sunlight before hitting the volcanic neck and sinking out of sight.

Silence hangs heavy in the air. A canyon wren warbles its laughing song. I listen, waiting to hear the sound that distinguishes Lava from every other rapid on the Colorado. The current, smooth as polished onyx, moves purposefully downstream like a messenger with an important document to deliver. Then I hear it—a faint roar that grows louder with each stroke until it dominates the air. Nothing of the turmoil creating the sound is visible. The river has vanished.

I watch in dismay as two rafts pull over to the left shore while the other four tie up on the right. I've never run left.

I turn *Sunshine Lady* and pull hard to the right, jump out, tie up and head up a well-worn trail around and over chunks of basalt. Silhouetted against a sapphire sky, people cluster, bent forward, pointing, conferring.

I join them at the lookout high above the rapid. It's worse than I remember, worse than I could have imagined. I search for the bubble line, a pathway that has proven on past trips to be as dependable as a train on a track. "Follow the bubbles, they know where they're going," a boatman told me on my first canyon trip.

The bubbles appear mysteriously, as if someone threw a stone into the exact same spot every few moments. They begin as a small disturbance on the surface fifty feet above the falls, then grow larger as they head into the rapid. First one, then two, then three. Three bubbles in a row on a direct and determined course through the Colorado's largest rapid. Right of the infamous ledge hole and left of a wild white ride. No room for error on a bubble run: a slot no more than ten feet across in a rapid that is nearly one hundred yards wide.

Since the bubbles first appear a short distance above the falls, and there are no other markers to sight on, to follow, to steady your failing nerves when you're on the river without the advantage of height that you had on the lookout, you are left alone, floating toward chaos in the middle of an ocean. Even after you locate the bubbles and are holding your boat directly over them, there's a moment—just before you slip over the brink—when you're sure you've miscalculated, for the bubbles lead into a wave that curls back like the paw of a grizzly ready to strike. Blind faith seems to be the only option. Hoping you haven't made a grave mistake, you lean hard on the oars and push into that first wave with every ounce of strength you've got. And when you're through that wall of water you push again, toward a gnarly reversed V-wave, then again into a twenty-foot wall of water that casts its own shadow, then again through the tail waves at the end of the rapid. Knees shaking, arms weak, you look back upstream and scream. A scream that reaches down to your solar plexus and releases the tension that has held you in its grip for days.

The bubbles form today, as always. But instead of leading through the storm, they lead into water that moves in every possible direction without form or order—whitewater that could take me and my boat and twist us inside out.

The train is derailed.

I look frantically at the far side of the river where the rapid is calmer, but only by comparison. A smooth tongue, complete with bubbles, leads into a reversed V-wave that looks runnable. A neat entry followed by outright madness.

Two of the boatmen return from scouting, shaking their heads. "It's too big to run."

"What will we do?" a passenger asks.

"We may have to portage. We could wait for the water to drop."

Dismal choices.

Discussion stops, as our attention is drawn to the other side of the river where the small party pushes away from shore. Carefully maneuvering his boat with an almost motionless sculling of the oars, the boatman edges the raft to the top of a slot, then shoots over the lip and into the whitewater. With just a few strokes, he glides the raft down a smooth strip of current, between holes and rocks, into the eddy below. He has run the unrunnable and made it look easy.

The second boat follows, a little askew, into a hole that crumples it in half. People fall into one another while the oars launch out of the boatwoman's hands. She quickly regains balance, recovers the oars and joins the first boat in the large eddy.

Lava is possible to run. One way or another, it is possible. Our party files off the lookout point back to the boats. As I start to leave, one of the guides stops me.

"I'm glad you're with us," he says.

"So am I."

"Don't get me wrong," he continues, "I think what you're doing is great, but today Lava deserves some extra safety."

A shiver of fear hits the pit of my stomach and causes me to tremble. I look again at the rapid and wonder what I would have done if I were here alone. I wouldn't have seen the left run. I might have gone through those monstrous holes and waves. Might have knocked myself senseless, might have suffered more harm than just flipping my raft. Yes, I'm glad they're here.

My run is anticlimactic: water rising and falling, seething and gushing, moving in a drenched insanity. I'm a fool seeking to create harmony out of disorder. With a final bounce it is over.

The boats mill around, a flotilla of energized people.

"Can I camp with you tonight?" I ask. It's not a time

to be alone.

"You bet," one of the boatmen answers.

We speed on down to a large, open camp. When the boats are settled against the shore, a boatman jumps aboard my boat and hands me a shot glass filled with tequila while he holds a beer ready in his other hand. "Here's to a good run at Lava." Down one, swallow a swig or two of the other. My insides are ablaze.

After dinner we cluster around a fire that thrusts back the sable night. Lava stories abate; we lapse into a comfortable silence. Then, against the backdrop of sand hills that border the camp, a light appears, minuscule at first, soon growing in size. In a moment we see a man dressed in loincloth and headband, his chest painted with streaks of red and black, silver bangles fluttering off his arms and lower legs. He holds a flaming torch high above his head.

He stops when he reaches the center of the group, peers at each of us and begins to speak slowly, voice husky and hesitating, each word deliberately measured, yet flowing.

"I am the Spirit of the Canyon and I have come here to tell you that I am pleased with you. You have given my chasms and cliffs and thundering waters the reverence they deserve;

you have not challenged my rapids in a contest of might, but have instead seen them as a pathway to knowledge; you have tended my beaches and plants and animals with care; you have played and rejoiced in me; you have understood that I am greater than all other places upon Mother Earth. Continue to care for my great expanses, and when you disperse, share with others the beauty you have gleaned within my depths, until everyone all over the land knows me and understands my greatness. This is not an idle thing I speak of, for I must be protected from heinous beings who seek to destroy me. I am pleased with you, as are all the other spirits of the canyon, and I bid you to continue on your journey in love."

He raises the torch, then turns and runs back to the sand dunes, leaving our small group in awe.

12

Coming Home

The most important thing is to hold on, hold out, for your creative life, for your solitude, for your time to be and do, for your very life. . . .

— *Clarissa Pinkola Estés, Ph.D.,*
Women Who Run With the Wolves

T he morning bustles with group activity. Everyone moves in different directions: packing bags, eating breakfast, scanning the beach for possessions overlooked. More than twenty people scurry here and there, emerging as a single unit, tied together by a cord of desire to move on downriver.

I hold back, leaving my sleeping bag stretched out on the sand, my bags unpacked. I have plenty of time to load my boat after the group departs, or to nap away the weariness resulting from a night without silence, not the silence of the previous nights when I could not hear someone breathing heavily or moving about restlessly with insomnia.

Finally the boats pull away from shore. We wave like strangers, knowing we'll never meet again.

I return to my night's camp and slowly, deliberately, stuff my sleeping bag in its sack, roll up my Therm-A-Rest, and fold my ground cloth. Each action takes an inordinate amount of energy.

The river flows in gentle riffles, almost as if she has spent herself in Lava and must take a rest. I feel as indolent as she and glide along with the easy flow. A mile or so downstream I see a group of hikers carrying heavy packs and walking sticks, making their way slowly over and among the rocks and cacti. I wave and float by, happy I don't have to expend such energy to reach my next camp. I stop for the day at Parashant Wash, a large beach with an abundant supply of driftwood and a stash of Coors beer, some of which an animal has punctured with claws or teeth. Somewhere in the vicinity a drunken ringtail prowls.

The following morning dark clouds spit like cats in a fight. I'm not inclined to move far from the campfire, to do more than wrap my hands around a cup of coffee and own the thoughts that swirl in my head.

For years I have been consumed by a burning desire to be a canyon guide. On my very first trip, when Babe was born, I learned that running rivers was the marrow of my existence. From the beginning, Mother River cradled me in white-capped hands, counseling me on a path of growth and self-discovery. Guiding was a natural extension, allowing me to spend whole summers floating rivers. It also permitted me to honor my individuality, to gain a sense that I was doing something worthwhile for myself, as well as for my passengers. As I grew more competent, my confidence and self-assurance grew stronger. I liked myself better than I ever had before, and I soon found my identity tightly tied up with being a river guide.

Now, however, I am full of questions about continuing to pursue work in the canyon. After spending more than twenty days alone on the river and a night with a commercial trip, I'm not sure I'm cut out for guiding anymore. I have serious doubts about being at other people's beck and call twenty-four hours a day, about the hard physical work, about taking flak for choosing a safe route through a rapid rather than the hair run. I'm not sure I want to entertain people who have paid a lot of money for their trip and expect a performance in return.

I take a gulp of lukewarm coffee and let these thoughts settle over me. Sometimes we crave things that are detrimental to our well-being. It is a peculiarly human perversity to desire a lover, a place or a job that is totally unsuited to us. We are willing to forego our very nature in order to gain what we want. Like trying to be an Afghan when we're actually a Golden Retriever. Can you imagine a lion wanting to be a cheetah, or a chimp hanging out with gorillas? Of course not. But we humans do it all the time. We do it to gain beauty, prestige, power or some other quality that is universally attractive. We think that by taking this person as our lover, or being hired for that job, or living in this place, we will be enhanced in some way. We will gain stature.

But intense longing also diminishes judgment and camouflages the flaws of an idea, person or job. What we desire has no imperfections; it is an impressionist painting with muted tones and soft edges. The hard lines revealing the truth are missing.

I wonder if I am deceiving myself by longing for this

river and this canyon. It could be that pursuing work in the canyon is wrong for me. I enjoy sharing special places with people, but not on demand. Rather than keeping up a lively conversation throughout the day, I often prefer silence. The best guides are usually extroverted, effervescent and dynamic. I am none of these things, and if I try to alter myself to work in the canyon, it could ultimately damage my psyche. I would be returning to a time before Babe, a time when I disowned myself to please others. If it were possible, I would spend months at a time in the canyon, but not necessarily with other people. The sacredness of solitude has grown large these past weeks; even with the closest of friends it would be lost. It is unrealistic to think I can enjoy being here with other boaters who load cases of beer and a boombox on their raft or with passengers who want a Disneyland experience.

A tight knot of fear and hurt overwhelms me. Working on the Colorado may be the only way I can gain regular access to Grand Canyon. The thought of turning my back on the canyon, of renouncing the opportunity to spend months on the river every year, of giving up a lifestyle that embraces creativity, individuality and freedom, makes me

weak, as if a large part of me is being extinguished. I shudder.
I am as stuck as I was on that ledge upriver, unhappy with
where I am, but afraid to move forward into an unknown
world.

I push the thoughts aside and shove off. The clouds tighten
up and a strong upriver wind slows my progress. Heavy rain
and hunger pangs hit simultaneously. I reach for a thermos.
Tea and chocolate fudge cookies. Nirvana on a cold, rainy
afternoon. I survey the passing scenery, wishing I had more
time to explore the numerous side canyons I pass.

The rain abates, the wind dies down. I should continue
but instead stop at Granite Park, only ten miles from Parashant
Wash. Not enough miles for the day. I'm already a day late in
passing Diamond Creek. In order to reach Pearce Ferry on
schedule, tomorrow must be a long river day. I set up a
minimal camp, prepare a cold dinner out of leftovers and
read and write inside my tent while a deluge drenches the
world outside.

With the new day, great cumulus clouds of white and
gray move across the sky like speeded-up images on a motion picture screen. Small patches of blue poke holes between
the fluff, promising clear skies. I walk away from camp and

discover hidden flowers and pregnant crystals of water hanging off leaves, ready to drop and destroy themselves on the thirsty earth. An alluvial plain dotted with cacti and the slender, graceful ocotillo stretches up to the cliffs, their mesas and buttes holding council away from the river. Large side canyons slash through hard walls, their corridors open, inviting me to walk along their pebble-strewn floors. Deep cloud shadows cloak a number of buttes in darkness, while others are bathed in full sunlight. Reluctantly I leave Granite Park, caught in a conflict of opposing desires—the need to push on and the wish to prolong my stay indefinitely.

I congratulate myself on an excellent run through 217 Mile Rapid, then enter the lower granite gorge. This is the third and last intrusion of the Vishnu Schist and Zoroaster Granite that remains at river level well after Lake Mead has drowned the exuberant Colorado.

I nod to nobody at a deserted Diamond Creek, the customary take-out for nearly all commercial companies and many private trips. I'm going all the way to Pearce Ferry in order not to miss the last fifteen miles of river or the forty-mile row across Lake Mead. A small price to pay to see the entire canyon and wind down slowly, instead of jumping abruptly into the outside world.

I stop briefly at Travertine Canyon and climb up the steep bank covered with large, smooth boulders to visit yet another place infused with magic and monkey flowers. Fresh water slides down a smooth wall and ferns grow in thick profusion on the side of a steep bank. I climb up the waterslide into a grotto, shadowy with eerie light and a waterfall that tumbles out of a hole at the top of the walls. A sacrosanct chamber of light and water and glistening black rock. Water falling, hitting stone, light reflected through silver drops, water speaking, breathing peace into me. When I leave this place, will something of my essence remain clinging to its walls? I want to believe that the spirits who inhabit this place will remember me as I remember them.

The day has slipped away into late afternoon. I stop for the night at Travertine Falls. Early the next morning I dress in my warmest clothes and go outside to greet the somber dawn.

A half-mile from camp I approach the first of the half-dozen rapids, which kick and scream and proclaim that while they might be tucked away at the end of the canyon, they are still to be reckoned with. I give them respect; they give me safe passage.

The river calms. Fluted rocks worn in beautiful patterns by wind and water, cacti that cling precariously to rocks, towering cliffs, the sensuous movement of the river all beckon me to linger. I imbibe my surroundings like a person dying of thirst, wishing to satiate my memory so I may relive this time over and over again when I have left the canyon behind.

Drifting by Separation Canyon sobers me. The backwaters of Lake Mead have stilled the river, though a thin line of current refuses to die. Six miles later I stop at Spencer Canyon. I follow trails that soon end at the base of a cliff or in the brackish water of the reservoir. No hiking here.

I set up camp, start a fire with wet wood and study a large chunk of lava across the river. A tombstone for Lava Cliff Rapid, the final testimony to a drop reputed to have been larger and more fearsome than Lava Falls, until Hoover Dam created Lake Mead and buried it.

I sit by the sputtering campfire, the moment infused with loneliness. Everything is different. The beach is more mud than sand, the trees droop in despondency, the slap of beaver tails echoes in the night. Mother River is drowned, Father Canyon's veins are clogged with a cancerous, foul water.

Gone is the gurgle and murmur of the river, gone is the life-giving force.

This is the loneliness I dreaded before my journey began, the loneliness I expected as a daily companion. I was fortunate that it only touched me lightly when I was upstream. Now that death surrounds me, and the outside world is imminent, loneliness takes root.

I'm not ready to return. I need to begin the trip over again. There is still so much to learn. And I haven't found Babe yet. I don't want to go back to the "real" world without her.

Then, with an imperceptible shift in perception, I know that I am wrong. Babe is with me—the two of us are inseparable. We have grown into one person. Even if I never return to Mother River and Father Canyon again, I won't lose her. As long as I remain true to myself, I remain faithful to her. Only dishonesty can chase her away now.

I look upriver and watch a faint glow fade from the uppermost cliffs. With the darkness, memories sweep over me: the camps, the rapids, the feelings of elation and despondency, the people I met and most of all the spirituality that touched me between these hallowed walls. Once again

Mother River and Father Canyon have looked after me. They have brought Babe home to me. They have helped me meet the challenge of facing myself day after day and accepting the risk of knowing myself, of opening up to my own vulnerability.

I don't know what lies ahead, and the thought of never seeing the canyon again may always fill me with pain. I do know I must let go of my need for it, to remember that often when we desire something too much, we inadvertently push it away. By letting the canyon go, it may come to me, and if it doesn't the wrongfulness of it will be apparent sometime in the future. Most of all, I need to listen to Babe, who knows everything there is to know, everything that is clear and right for me.

It is time to move on. My search for freedom has led me into a trap. It is only through commitment—first to myself then perhaps to another—that I can ever know complete freedom.

I stir the fire and spread out the coals. The loneliness evaporates, replaced by a sense of security and accomplishment. I'd like to believe I only have a little farther to travel before I can row every rapid in life perfectly. I smile. I've learned enough to know that once started, growing doesn't stop. Life is very much like a river trip. Some days I'll have perfect runs, and other days I'll eddy out and flounder around in murky water before continuing on downstream. But unlike in the past, now *I'm* the one at the oars.

The next morning I board *Sunshine Lady* for the final haul across Lake Mead. It begins to rain, and the drops strike the water with such force that a company of sprites dances on the river. With a laugh, I jump on top of the ammo boxes and do my own dance. I turn my face to the sky as the raindrops turn into a shower of rose petals while the assembly of sprites whirls around me in celebration. "I did it!" I throw out my arms to the thronging crowds, "I did it!" The sprites dance even harder. *"Yes! I did it!"*

About the Author

Patricia C. McCairen left her native New York City when she discovered whitewater rafting on a trip down the Colorado River through Grand Canyon. She has been rafting for more than twenty years, and worked as a guide for five years. She is the author of *River Runners' Recipes* (Menasha Ridge Press, 1994) and has written a novel and a number of short stories. A seasoned traveler, she has been to more than twenty countries and all seven continents.

Adventura is a popular line of books from Seal Press that celebrates the achievements and experiences of women adventurers, athletes, travelers and naturalists. Please peruse the list of books below—and discover the spirit of adventure through the female gaze.

SOLO: *On Her Own Adventure,* edited by Susan Fox Rogers. $12.95, 1-878067-74-5.

ANOTHER WILDERNESS: *Notes from the New Outdoorswoman,* edited by Susan Fox Rogers. $16.00, 1-878067-30-3.

FEMME D'ADVENTURE: *Travel Tales from Inner Montana to Outer Mongolia,* by Jessica Maxwell. $14.00, 1-878067-98-2.

ALL THE POWERFUL INVISIBLE THINGS: *A Sportswoman's Notebook,* by Gretchen Legler. $12.95, 1-878067-69-9.

SEASON OF ADVENTURE: *Traveling Tales and Outdoor Journeys of Women Over 50,* edited by Jean Gould. $15.95, 1-878067-81-8.

A DIFFERENT ANGLE: *Fly Fishing Stories by Women,* edited by Holly Morris. $22.95, cloth, 1-878067-63-X.

UNCOMMON WATERS: *Women Write About Fishing,* edited by Holly Morris. $16.95, 1-878067-76-1.

LEADING OUT: *Women Climbers Reaching for the Top,* edited by Rachel da Silva. $16.95, 1-878067-20-6.

THE CURVE OF TIME, by M. Wylie Blanchet. $12.95, 1-878067-27-3.

RIVERS RUNNING FREE: *A Century of Women's Canoeing Adventures,* edited by Judith Niemi and Barbara Wieser. $16.95, 1-878067-90-7.

WATER'S EDGE: *Women Who Push the Limits in Rowing, Kayaking and Canoeing,* by Linda Lewis. $14.95, 1-878067-18-4.

ORDERING INFORMATION

If you are unable to obtain a Seal Press title from a bookstore, please order from us directly. Checks, MasterCard and Visa accepted. Enclose payment with your order and 16.5% of the book total for shipping and handling. Washington residents should add 8.6% sales tax. Send to:

Orders Dept., Seal Press, 3131 Western Avenue, Suite 410, Seattle, WA 98121

1-800-754-0271 orders only / (206) 283-7844 / fax: (206) 285-9410 sealprss@scn.org. Visit our website at http://www.sealpress.com